# Lemon
# Magic

D0095761

# Lem🍋n Magic

## 200 Beauty and Household Uses for Lemons and Lemon Juice

### PATTY MOOSBRUGGER

THREE RIVERS PRESS

NEW YORK

Published by Three Rivers Press, New York, New York. Member of the Crown Publishing Group.

Random House, Inc. New York, Toronto, London, Sydney, Auckland
www.randomhouse.com

THREE RIVERS PRESS is a registered trademark and the Three Rivers Press colophon is a trademark of Random House, Inc.

Printed in the United States of America

Design by Howard P. Johnson

Library of Congress Cataloging-in-Publication Data

Moosbrugger, Patty.
    Lemon magic : 200 beauty and household uses for lemons and lemon juice / Patty Moosbrugger. — 1st ed.
       p.    cm.
    Includes index.
    1. Home economics.  2. Lemon.  3. Lemon juice  4. House cleaning.
    I. Title.
    TX158.M657   1999
650'.41—dc21                               98-28900
                                            CIP

ISBN 0-609-80340-9 (pbk.)

10 9 8 7 6 5 4 3

First Edition

*For my little lemondrop, Madeline*

# Contents

# *Author's Note*

The author has included cautions and general guidelines for using lemons in this book. However, each individual, fabric, or material may react differently to a particular suggested use. For this reason, the author cannot assume responsibility for personal or property damage resulting from the use of the suggestions found here. It is recommended that before you begin to use any suggestion, you read the directions carefully. With respect to the use of lemons on fabric or any other material, test it first in a small, inconspicuous place. If you have any questions or concerns regarding the safety or health effects of any suggestions, consult first with a physician or other appropriate professional.

# Lemons
# Past and
# Present

While nobody can say for sure just where or when lemons were discovered, there is evidence that the precious fruit was first used by the ancient people who inhabited the subcontinent of India more than two thousand years before the birth of Christ. The cradle of civilization in India was located at a site known as Mohenjo Daro in the Indus River Valley, in what is now Pakistan. This highly developed society is estimated to have existed as far back in history as 2500 B.C., and its people were among the very first human beings to admire and appreciate lemons. We know that to be true because an earring, clearly shaped in the form of a lemon, was found at an archaeological site in the Mohenjo Daro region. The lemon's exact usage by the inhabitants of Mohenjo Daro is shrouded in mystery and we cannot now know whether or not these ancient people valued the lemon for its delicate aroma, flavor, or its medicinal properties. No seeds were found, and archaeologists can only speculate about the way in which lemons were used by these people in the distant past.

Throughout history, the presence of lemons in different ancient societies and how they were utilized is a subject open to wide speculation. For centuries and centuries after the lemon's first appearance in ancient India, there remains no trace of it in either archaeological excavations or recorded history. It would be more than two thousand years after the time of Mohenjo Daro before we would again find evidence of lemons.

After such a long absence, lemons appeared in ancient Greece in the fifth century B.C. The Greeks knew of lemons as "Median apples," named after the ancient country of Media, located in what is now the western portion of Iran. Although the lengthy time gap between these two appearances of the lemon is surprising, the geographical distance is not particularly great, and it is easy to imagine how the far-roaming Greeks would have discovered lemons. The Greeks maintained contacts throughout Central Asia and, because of their travels to Media, took notice of lemons and mentioned them in their theatrical and botanical writings. Aristophanes, the great Greek playwright of comedies, wrote about the lemon in the fifth century B.C., and Theophrastus, a Greek philosopher and botanist, also wrote of Median apples about a hundred years later.

The spread of lemons westward can be seen afterward in the writings of ancient Romans a few hundred years later. The poet Virgil (70–19 B.C.), who had studied the literature of the Greeks, referred to lemons as Median apples in his poetry. The Romans realized the medicinal powers of lemons; Virgil exclaimed that the lemon tree was the best antidote to all poisons and one of the richest products of Media. Hundreds of years later, around A.D. 300, Athenaeus, a well-known scholar and author of his time, also illustrated the Roman belief that the lemon was an antidote to all poisons. He told of two criminals who were thrown into a pit with venomous snakes. One of the prisoners had eaten a lemon beforehand. He survived the venomous bite of the snake, while the criminal who had not eaten the lemon succumbed to the bite and died promptly thereafter.

Sometime around the birth of Christ, the elusive fruit appeared in the writings of the famous Roman poet Ovid. He is the man who chronicled the twelve labors of the mighty Hercules. Anyone who has read his account of the hero's tasks will remember well that in the last of Hercules' twelve labors, his

task was to steal the "golden apples" from the Hesperides. It is claimed by some that these golden
apples were actually lemons; later some ancient
writers referred to lemons as "Hesperides apples."
But if these fruits Ovid refers to were really what we
now know as lemons, they were certainly still a rare
fruit in the ancient Mediterranean world—2,500
years after our first sighting of lemons in ancient
India. For in that twelfth labor of Hercules, the fruits
were so rare and special that they grew on a tree
guarded by a terrible dragon. The garden belonged
to the Hesperides, the "daughters of night," who
lived near Mount Atlas. Certainly such a tale would
not have been invented about a common fruit.

Though rare in the Roman Empire, the fruit was
well enough known there not only to have been
included in the writings of Virgil and Athenaeus but
even to have been depicted by painters of walls and
makers of mosaics in Pompeii. It also began showing up in mural paintings by the fourth century A.D.
It was around then that the Roman agricultural
writer Palladius was credited with having planted
the first lemon tree in Italy. With the fall of the
Roman empire in the late fifth century, however, the
sporadic cultivation of lemons, which probably was
taking place in the Mediterranean basin, was aban-

doned. There was no longer a market for the rare and expensive fruits.

During the eighth and ninth centuries, Arabs planted lemon trees in the Sahara Desert, and it was probably from this source that the North African Moors got their lemon trees. The Moors brought lemon trees to Europe when they invaded Spain in the eighth century. The Moors are credited with planting the lemon orchards of Andalusia, an area that remains one of the primary lemon-producing orchards in the world today. The Moors probably also started the orchards in Sicily, a country they also invaded, and it is from there that lemons made their way back into Italy a few hundred years after disappearing with the collapse of the Roman empire.

But while lemons seem to have been regularly cultivated in the dry, warm climates of North Africa, the Middle East, and Near East during the first millennium, it would still be many years before they were brought to Europe in any substantial quantities. Lemons wouldn't make it to the northern countries in Europe until the Crusaders brought them back from their travels to the Near East, sometime in the thirteenth century. In Paris during this time imported lemons started showing up in the markets, where they were sold by the *marchands d'aigrun,* merchants who had a monopoly on the citrus fruits (*aigrun* came from *aigre,* meaning *acid*). They were certainly an expensive luxury, however, and were not readily available to the masses.

In 1494 we know that Cesare Borgia, the Spanish-Italian prince and prototype for Machiavelli's *The Prince,* sent to his wife, who was being held in France by Louis XII, a wonderful selection of gifts that included both oranges and lemons. Although lemons were still quite unknown in France in the fifteenth century, Christopher Columbus was able to obtain them for his voyage to the New World in 1493. He deposited the lemons on the island of Hispaniola, which is now Haiti and the Dominican Republic, and from there the seeds traveled to nearby Florida. They must have done pretty well in the New World during the following century, because in 1579, eighty years after their introduction to North America, a healthy crop of lemons was growing in St. Augustine, Florida.

A few years later, during the reign of Louis XIV (1638–1715), lemons made their way into a few more French hands. We know this because the ladies of Louis XIV's court made a habit of occasionally biting lemons in order to keep their lips seductively red. Perhaps it gave them a nice little pucker as well.

While lemons were enhancing the sex appeal of beautiful French women of the aristocracy, men at sea in the eighteenth century were benefiting from their special health-enhancing qualities. The British Navy was including lemon juice in the rations of sailors to combat scurvy. This terrible disease had long affected sailors who spent days on end at sea without foods that contained the essential nutrient vitamin C. Its symptoms included swollen gums, tooth loss, loss of energy, and extreme weakness leading to gradual starvation. From the very beginning of the Age of Exploration, scurvy had claimed the lives of thousands of sailors. On Vasco da Gama's historic voyage in 1497 to India more than half his crew died of scurvy. Voyages often began in the early spring following long winters during which neither vegetables nor fruits were eaten by most Europeans. Not surprisingly, those who manned the ships were often in a state of rundown health even before they boarded their vessels. The long months at sea, with only biscuits and hard, dried meats for rations, caused them to succumb easily to illness as a result of vitamin-C deficiency.

The Chinese knew of the importance of fresh

fruits and vegetables as early as the fifth century and had long carried them on their oceangoing vessels. Their knowledge was passed on to the Dutch and the British who traveled in Asia, and in 1601 it is recorded that the British East India Company gathered oranges and lemons off the coast of Madagascar specifically for the purpose of preventing scurvy. This knowledge, however, was not universally known or accepted and there was much argument over what caused scurvy and what could be done to prevent it. Some thought it was the result of too much salt in the foods consumed while at sea. Others who knew that citrus worked as a preventative for scurvy looked for a cheaper and more readily available cure. Physicians thought that malt, sauerkraut, cider, or pickles might work, but since no one knew what it was in citrus that prevented scurvy, no satisfactory alternative was found and sailors continued to fall ill.

Finally, at the end of the eighteenth century, the British Admiralty decreed that the juice of citrus fruits was the only medicine that could conquer a disease that had been responsible for more sailors' deaths than any other cause, including the cannon fire of the enemy. A daily ration of lemon juice was added to the rum "grog" and over 1.6 million gallons of lemon juice were included in the rum rations between 1795 and 1815. The addition of lemon juice resulted in a dramatic decrease in deaths at sea. In the mid-nineteenth century, the British began to substitute lime juice from the West Indies for lemon juice, resulting in the term "limeys" for British seamen. Unfortunately, limes were not suitable replacements for lemons, nature's most potent and concentrated source of vitamin C, and proved much less effective against scurvy.

In the New World, the lemons that had been planted in St. Augustine in the late sixteenth century did not thrive long enough to make Florida the biggest citrus-producing state in the country. The reason is that lemons thrive most successfully in warm, semi-arid regions that experience light rainfall and low humidity. The humid climate of Florida causes lemons to be susceptible to fungal diseases. Consequently, it was an extremely difficult job for the early lemon growers in Florida to build a healthy, sustainable lemon industry there. When the majority of Florida's lemon trees were killed in a cold spell at the end of the nineteenth century, the growers basically gave up on the industry, yet continued to produce other citrus fruits, such as oranges and grapefruits, in large quantities. In the early

1950s, lemons were reintroduced to Florida, but the lemon industry in Florida today is small, producing lemons of lower quality that are used exclusively in lemon juice and lemonade.

Lemons found their way to the region that became California via Franciscan missionaries, who introduced them there in the eighteenth century. Despite the ideal semi-arid climate that was to be found in California, the initial varieties of lemons that these monks introduced did not thrive.

The scarcity of fresh lemons in the West became an issue of life or death during the California Gold Rush. In 1848, more than 40,000 prospectors made their way to California as a result of the discovery of gold at Sutter's Mill. The extreme lack of fresh produce in the area resulted in the manifestation of scurvy among miners in such large numbers that people were willing to pay a dollar per lemon in order to stave off the dreaded disease. As a result, farmers rushed to begin planting lemons and scores of orchards sprang up, forming the basis for what would later become one of the world's greatest lemon-growing regions.

By 1874, the hardier Lisbon variety of the fruit was introduced to California and became successfully established as the principal type of lemon grown in the dry, warm inland region. In 1878, the cooler, coastal areas of California saw the successful introduction of the Eureka variety. Today California is a grower of high-quality lemons and, in fact, is responsible for the production of one-third of the total global lemon crop.

Wherever they were introduced, lemons quickly became staples for cooks. They are, indeed, a funny food because though perceived as important for their unique qualities, they are almost never eaten by themselves. When lemons started appearing in Paris, their juice soon replaced verjuice (sour-grape juice), which was traditionally used in sauces requiring a little touch of acidity. In Italy, as early as 1474, lemon juice appeared in a cookbook as a suggested replacement for other spices. Lemons provided one of the first flavors for soda water in 1840 and have inspired countless desserts and dishes as a main flavor enhancer over the ages. Indeed, lemon-flavored desserts have been in vogue in the United States throughout the twentieth century and are as popular today as they ever were.

In the 1920s as refrigerators started replacing iceboxes, there arose a whole spate of new and easy recipes for "refrigerator dishes." In 1927, General Electric came out with a cookbook entitled

*Electric Refrigerator Recipes and Menus* and one popular recipe was for a lemony dessert called either Refrigerator Cake or Flapper Pudding. The recipe called for the layering of meringue, ladyfingers, and lemon curd to be finally topped with whipped cream and maraschino cherries. Once the puddings and cookies were layered on top of each other in their pan, you simply covered the pan and popped it in the refrigerator to chill for twelve hours.

What we now all know as lemon chiffon cake was quite a rage in its heyday in the 1940s. The cake was invented by a California salesman named Harry Baker in 1927, but he kept his recipe secret for many, many years. The dessert first became famous in Hollywood, where Mr. Baker made it for celebrity parties as a special and exclusive dish. He finally sold the recipe to General Mills in 1947, which posted gains of 20 percent on sales of cake flour after the recipe was published. Although lemon was the most popular flavor of chiffon cake from the start, it could be made with a number of other flavors, from orange to coconut.

With the advent of easy cooking and preprepared food in the 1950s, lemon sherbet became popular. Following a typical 1950s meal, which often included various combinations of frozen vegetables, canned mushrooms, and the ubiquitous and essential can of creamed soup that was used as flavoring, the gourmet way of topping it off would be a cup of lemon sherbet with a little creme de menthe poured over it. Though it was the liqueur that guaranteed its gourmet status, lemon sherbet was the ultimate choice for a fashionable dessert at a dinner party during this decade.

Lemon bars first made their appearance in *Betty Crocker's Cook Book* in 1963 and their popularity as a much-desired dessert continues in the present era. Everybody had a recipe for lemon bars in the 1970s, when they were at the height of their popularity. Today, you need look no further than the cake mix section of the grocery store to find a selection of boxed mixes for lemon bars, which now provide a quick and easy alternative for many household cooks in America to the made-from-scratch version.

Wouldn't the ancient Romans have been surprised to see their rare and prized lemon in such abundance?

# Making the Most of Your Lemons

With some care, your lemons can go a lot further than a squeeze or two, producing tasty lemon juice that you can use in all sorts of ways. A large lemon will yield up to 4 tablespoons of juice and 3 teaspoons of zest, much more than the average person uses when squeezing a bit of lemon into a cup of tea or flavoring a piece of fish. If you know the tricks for the most effective squeezing and the most economical freezing, each lemon will yield much more than expected.

The best lemons for juice and pulp are the small round or oval ones with smooth, unblemished skins. Large, coarse-skinned lemons are likely to have thick skin and relatively little flesh and juice. The fruits you pick should be firm, glossy, and bright. They should always be bright yellow and not greenish. Beware that the green-tinged lemons will tend to be more acidic. Heavy fruits with fine-grained skins are the juiciest. Avoid hard, shriveled lemons as well as spongy, soft ones.

Store lemons at room temperature in an airy basket if you are going to use them within a few days. You will obtain more juice from a lemon that is not cold. Lemons will keep at room temperature for about one week. If you intend to keep the lemons for some time, they must be refrigerated. Lemons can be stored in a plastic bag in the refrigerator for two to three weeks.

You should also be aware that lemons, lemon juice, and lemon zest can be frozen. So, if you only need half a lemon for a recipe, or if you find that you've bought more lemons than you can use, here are a number of tips for preserving those valuable lemons.

## PRESERVED LEMONS

*4 medium lemons*
*²/₃ cup kosher salt*
*1 tablespoon black peppercorns (optional) or one*
    *cinnamon stick (optional)*
*¹/₂ cup fresh lemon juice*
*Water*

You can use preserved lemons in a multitude of ways—in salsa, guacamole, seviche, rice, soups, salads, or in stewed or baked meat dishes, particularly lamb or chicken. If you cut them into strips, they also make a nice addition to Bloody Marys or martinis.

1. Cut lemons lengthwise in quarters. In a large bowl, combine lemons and salt, tossing to coat thoroughly. Layer the lemons, peppercorns or cinnamon stick (if desired) and salt in a 1½-quart glass or earthenware jar.

2. As you add the lemons, use a large spoon to press them down lightly to release their juices. Add lemon juice and just enough water to cover the lemons. Seal the jar tightly and refrigerate, unopened, for 2 to 3 weeks, shaking the jar daily. After this time, the lemons will keep in the refrigerator for months.

3. To use, rinse or scrape the salt off the lemon, scrape out and discard pulp and pith. Chop or slice the rind as desired.

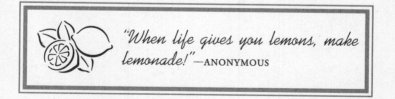

*"When life gives you lemons, make lemonade!"* —ANONYMOUS

21

# PRESERVED FROZEN
# LEMON WEDGES

You can cut an extra half lemon, or even a whole lemon, into slices and wrap the slices individually in plastic wrap and freeze them. These are wonderful to have on hand when you want a single slice of lemon for a cup of hot tea. You don't even need to thaw the slice before using it for your tea; simply drop the slice into the hot beverage.

## PRESERVING FRESH LEMON JUICE

You can squeeze all the juice out of one or more lemons and freeze it in small plastic containers or ice-cube trays. Lemon juice cubes are a wonderful addition to iced tea in the summer. Besides adding a delicious lemon flavor, these keep the drink cold longer without watering it down, as can happen with ice cubes. Once the lemon juice cubes have been frozen, simply transfer them to a plastic freezer bag for use anytime.

## PRESERVING LEMONS IN FRESH WATER

*I*f you can't use your lemons right away but don't want to freeze them, you can put them in an airtight, water-filled jar for longer freshness. Once you've placed the lemons in a jar, put the container in the refrigerator for later use. Lemons can keep for up to a month this way.

## MAKING LEMON ZEST

*T*o get zest from a lemon, you can always buy a fancy little tool called a lemon zester, which pares off the zest as its only function, or you can simply cut off strips of zest using a vegetable peeler. When getting zest, make sure to clean the lemons well beforehand to get all the chemical fertilizers off the skin. Then scrape off the outer portion of the peel—the zest—being careful to scrape only the outer skin. If you get the white pith along with the skin, it will be bitter and mar the flavor of the zest. Once you have removed the zest, finely chop.

## PRESERVING LEMON ZEST

*L*emon zest can be successfully preserved by either drying or freezing it. To dry lemon zest for later use, take the finely chopped zest and dry it in a single layer at room temperature overnight, or until completely dry. If you're in a hurry, place the grated zest on an ungreased baking sheet and bake at 200 degrees Fahrenheit for about 20 minutes, stirring occasionally. Cool zest completely before storing it in an airtight container at room temperature.

If you want to store your lemon zest in the freezer, wrap it in plastic wrap or aluminum foil and stow it away there. If you plan on making recipes that call for both rind and juice, mix the appropriate proportions of the two before freezing.

## MAKING GRANULATED
## LEMON ZEST

*L*emon zest can be sweetened and turned into granulated lemon zest to be used in all sorts of dishes. You can make granulated lemon zest by combining the outer peel (yellow portion only) of one lemon with 1 to 2 tablespoons of granulated sugar in a food processor fitted with a metal blade.

Process until the mixture is powdery and use the sugared zest in everything from tea to desserts.

## INCREASING THE AMOUNT OF LEMON JUICE

*T*o get the most juice out of a lemon, the fruit should be at room temperature or warmer; if need be, place it in hot water or a low-heated oven for a few minutes to warm it, or microwave it for 30 seconds. Then, roll the lemon a couple of times firmly between your palm and the countertop until it feels softened.

Another way to increase the amount of juice is to prick the skin in several places (don't penetrate the flesh) and microwave on High for 10 to 20 seconds. Let a microwaved lemon stand for one minute before rolling it on the countertop and squeezing.

## KEEPING JUICE LEMONS FOR LATER

*I*f you have a recipe that calls for only a little lemon juice and you don't want to cut a whole lemon apart and render much of it useless, you would be wise to pierce the lemon with a fork and squeeze out just the right amount of juice. Afterward, store the lemon in a plastic bag for later use. You can also pierce the lemon with toothpicks in several places, and leave the toothpicks in the holes. They will function as plugs and prevent the juice from drying out while it is stored in the refrigerator.

## REVIVING HARDENED LEMONS

*I*f you find that your lemons have hardened from standing for too long, they can easily be revived. Simply take the hardened lemons and place them in boiling water that just covers the lemons. Then remove the pan from the heat and let the lemons stand for a few moments before using them.

# Lemons:
# The Household
# Alternative

We all know the popular saying, "When life gives you lemons, make lemonade." As it turns out, however, lemonade is certainly not the only thing that can be made with lemons. If life gives you lemons, you can make myriad products, from nail whitener to hairspray, from a flea exterminator to a brass cleaner. Lemons come in handy not only for flavoring soups and replacing salt but for cleaning the bathroom or amusing the kids in the playroom. They act as a safe alternative to some toxic household cleaners and are a natural substitute for all sorts of medicines, from cough syrups to heartburn relievers. You might even find that lemons can replace a missing ingredient when you're mixing up a batch of cookie dough. Grated lemon rind, after all, can be used in place of vanilla extract if you find yourself in a jam.

As we find ourselves ever more surrounded by toxic household solutions and fancy specialty cleaners for everything from leather to metal, it is nice to know that we can do the same things with a mixture of common household ingredients and lemons. There is almost no scent so fresh and clean smelling as a lemon, and you don't have to buy chemical-laden products to get that. (Most products that boast lemon scent, in fact, have no lemons at all but a combination of chemicals to create the scent artificially.)

Lemons are also wonderful substitutes for the many specialty health and beauty products we find ourselves faced with on pharmacy shelves. After all, who wouldn't prefer to give their child a mixture of natural lemon and honey if they knew it would achieve the same results as the expensive cough medicine they find themselves worrying over.

So, when you have a need for a specialty cleaning product or health and beauty product, or even when you just want a good strong cleaner for countertops or bathroom surfaces, you probably need look no further than the fruit bowl on your countertop or the fruit drawer in your refrigerator. If you have some lemons on hand, they just may be able to produce that magic touch you are looking for.

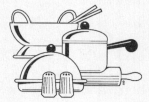

# *In the Kitchen*

## ZESTY LEMON TARTS AND PIES

*I*f you want to add some zest to your lemon tarts or pies, try rubbing a sugar cube over the surface of a lemon. The sugar cube will extract oils from the lemon that will be released during the cooking process. This trick works for oranges, too.

## ALUMINUM COOKWARE CLEANER

*L*emon juice can be used effectively to remove interior discoloration that mars the surface of your aluminum cookware. This can be achieved by filling the discolored pan with water and lemon juice. Add one tablespoon of lemon juice per quart of water and simmer until the discoloration is gone. Complete the task by scouring with a steel wool pad.

## BERRY-STAINED HANDS CLEANER

*S*tubborn berry and other fruit stains can be easily removed with lemon juice. Simply rub a teaspoon or two of lemon juice into the stained area of your hands and finish up by washing as usual.

## KITCHEN COUNTERTOP CLEANER

*L*emon juice really works well as a cleaning aid for all sorts of stains that mar the surface of your kitchen counters and cabinets. Apply lemon juice to the entire countertop or cabinet front and let it soak into the surface for about half an hour. Then sprinkle baking soda on a clean cloth and gently scrub the affected areas. You'll see that the stains will disappear and your kitchen will also smell great afterward.

## COFFEE CARAFE CLEANER

*W*aiters and waitresses have long used lemon juice to quickly remove burned-in coffee residue from the bottoms of coffee carafes. Just fill the coffeepot with two tablespoons salt, enough ice to cover the bottom of the pot, and the juice of one quartered lemon along with the lemon wedges themselves, and swirl the contents in a circular motion until the coffee stains lift from the glass surface. This method works amazingly well to remove even the most tarry coffee stains in no time at all. Finish up by cleaning the carafe as usual with dishwashing detergent and warm water.

## COOKED CABBAGE ODOR REMOVER

*C*abbage is such a healthy food to eat, but it can really make the kitchen a smelly place while it is cooking. Lemon can help lessen the odor of cooking cabbage and improve the taste at the same time. Just put half a lemon into the water when cooking cabbage and you'll find that it will keep the smell from filling the kitchen. It's important to note that overcooking cabbage makes the smell worse and decreases the nutritional content as well.

## FRESH POULTRY
## DEODORIZER

*F*or those who object to the odor of uncooked chicken, duck, goose, or any type of wild fowl, lemon works well to freshen these birds. Massage the plucked poultry with the juice of ¹/₂ lemon and ¹/₄ teaspoon of salt. This will eliminate the odor of uncooked poultry and improve the taste of the skin after the poultry has been cooked.

## BAKING SODA FRESHNESS
## DETECTOR

*B*aking soda can work all sorts of wonders, but not if it is too old to be effective. If the freshness of your baking soda is in question, lemon can quickly determine whether or not it is still in good shape. Just add one teaspoon of lemon juice to a pinch of baking soda. If it bubbles, the baking soda is still in good shape and will work fine as a deodorizer or cleaning agent. If it doesn't bubble up after adding the lemon juice, then it's time to change the box in your refrigerator or cupboard.

## DICING DRIED FRUIT MADE EASY

*I*f you need to cut up dried fruit and find that the knife keeps on sticking to it, try using a little lemon juice to make the task easier. Before dicing the dried fruit, drizzle a bit of lemon juice over the knife to make the job go more smoothly.

## CHOPPING BOARD
## STAIN REMOVER

*F*rom grease stains to vegetable and fruit stains, lemon can help you to restore discolored chopping boards to their original color. Simply rub the chopping board with lemon juice until the stains come out. Your chopping board will look much better—and smell better, too.

## FISH FLAVOR ENHANCER

*L*emon juice rubbed on fish before cooking will enhance the flavor and help maintain a good color. Squeeze the juice of a lemon evenly over the surface of the fish right before cooking. If you are baking fish in aluminum foil or a covered oven roaster, add cut lemon slices and fresh herbs or

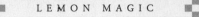

other seasonings before baking to improve the taste
of oven-cooked fish.

## FIRMING POACHED FISH

*I*f you prefer your fish or other seafoods
poached, the addition of a bit of lemon juice to
the poaching liquid will help maintain the original
consistency of the fresh seafood while cooking and
result in a firmer and whiter (or pinker, in the case
of salmon) cooked fish upon serving. Add the juice
of half a lemon per pound of seafood to the poaching solution before cooking.

## MAKING FLAKIER,
## CRISPER PASTRY

*C*hefs differ on their approaches to adding
lemon juice to pastries for a crispier and
flakier finish, but they all agree that lemon juice is a
must for the best pie crusts and other pastries. You
can try each of these different approaches and
choose your favorite:

Substitute one tablespoon of very cold lemon
juice for one tablespoon ice water, or

Add one tablespoon powdered milk to the flour
and use ice-cold water and a squeeze of
lemon juice, or

Add one tablespoon of lemon juice to the batter.

## MAKING FLUFFIER
## RICE

*F*or fluffier, whiter rice, add one teaspoon of
lemon juice per quart of water before cooking
your rice. The lemon juice will also prevent the rice
from sticking together and add a flavor that will
complement many types of dishes.

## GARBAGE DISPOSAL
## FRESHENER

*T*he natural deodorizing properties of lemons
can be put to use even after the juice has been
squeezed out of the fruit. A great way to both get
rid of your leftover lemon rinds and freshen your
garbage disposal at the same time is to use the discarded lemon rinds as garbage disposal cleaners.
Place ice and used lemon peels in the garbage disposal and grind away. Besides freshening the disposal, the ice will clean and sharpen the blades.

## JAM-MAKING HINT

*A*dd the juice of one lemon to almost any jam or jelly recipe while it is cooking. The addition of lemon juice improves the appearance of your favorite jam or jelly by helping to maintain the fruit's original color and makes for faster jelling of your favorite preserve.

## KEEPING BEETS FROM FADING

*I*f you find that your beets lose their color when boiled, add a little lemon juice to the water. You'll see that the beets will retain their original bright magenta throughout the cooking process.

## KEEPING EGGSHELLS FROM CRACKING

*L*emon can help to keep boiled eggs from cracking during the cooking process. Just rub the cut side of a lemon half over the eggshell surface before boiling.

# REMOVING GARLIC AND ONION ODORS FROM HANDS

*L*emons can be used to remove the stubborn odors of garlic and onion from hands after handling these foods. Rub your hands with a piece of cut lemon or the juice from a lemon, and make certain to get the juice under the nails and around the cuticles. Follow by rinsing hands with water.

## GARLIC BREATH REMEDY

*I*f you enjoy Italian food or other cuisines that use a lot of garlic but find that the taste lingers on a bit longer than you would like, try using lemon—with a little spice—as a natural breath freshener. Just crush one or two cloves into a hot lemon drink and swirl the mixture around in your mouth before swallowing.

## PERFECTING HARD-BOILED EGGS

*A*dd to the water in which you boil eggs one teaspoon of lemon juice or a small piece of lemon. The eggshells will peel off more easily.

## KEEPING CUT FRUIT FROM TURNING BROWN

When preparing cut fruit ahead of time for a fruit salad or other purpose, add lemon juice immediately upon slicing the fruit so that it will not brown or darken. The juice of $1/2$ lemon should be enough for a quart or two of cut fruit. If you want to use only half of an avocado, apple, pear, banana, or other type of fresh fruit, rub a section of lemon or lemon juice over the remaining half immediately upon cutting it, then cover and refrigerate.

## KEEPING GUACAMOLE GREEN

The next time you're planning a Mexican fiesta and want to make your guacamole in advance but are worried about it turning an ugly shade of brown in the middle of your party, don't forget to have your lemon juice on hand. After preparing your guacamole, drizzle enough lemon juice over the surface to lightly cover it. The vibrant green of the avocado will be preserved for much longer as a result.

## KEEPING MUSHROOMS WHITE AND FIRM WHEN SAUTÉING

*T*o keep mushrooms white and firm while sautéing, add a teaspoon of lemon juice to each quarter pound of butter. As long as you don't overcook mushrooms, they will be much less likely to shrivel up and turn brown.

## KEEPING SWEET CORN YELLOW

*T*o keep sweet corn yellow, add one teaspoon of lemon juice to the cooking water about a minute before taking it off the stove. This will also help to keep the corn firm and prevent it from becoming mushy.

## KEEPING WHITE VEGGIES WHITE

*L*emon juice will help cauliflower, potatoes, kohlrabi, white radishes, or any other white vegetable to stay white even after they have been cooked. Add one teaspoon of lemon juice to the cooking water to keep the cauliflower, potatoes, or other white vegetables white.

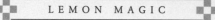

## FRESHER GREENS TIP

*L*emon can help to keep spinach, mustard, collard, or any other type of greens fresher and crisper. Add a few drops of lemon juice to the water before washing your greens. Doing so will crispen the greens and help remove dirt, sand, and any bugs or slugs that may be hiding within the folds of the greens.

## MICROWAVE OVEN CLEANER

*I*f you find that the smells from your microwave oven are not going away after a regular cleaning with soap and water, use lemon juice to do the job. Add the juice of half a lemon to one cup water and heat in the microwave on High for one minute. Then keep the door closed for a few minutes, and, finally, wipe the interior dry. The lingering odors will have disappeared.

 *The average orchard yield per lemon tree is 1,500 lemons in one year.*

## REMOVING NONSTICK-PAN STAINS

*N*onstick cookware is a great invention, but the delicate nature of the surface of these pots and pans makes them difficult to clean well because you can't scour them with abrasive cleaners. If you have a stubborn stain, use 2 to 3 tablespoons of baking soda mixed with enough water to cover the area of the pan and add one slice of lemon. Put the pan on the stove top and simmer the mixture until the stain disappears. (Be careful not to let the liquid boil off.)

## PERKING UP GREEN VEGETABLES

*I*t's really surprising how a little bit of lemon juice added to fresh cool water can really revitalize vegetables that look like they are headed for the garbage can instead of the dinner table. Add a teaspoon of lemon juice to each half gallon of cool water and then place the vegetables in the water. Vegetables that have stems, such as broccoli and asparagus, should be cut at the bottom; other vegetables, such as green peppers, should be cut or chopped to expose the most surface before placing them in the cool water. It usually takes 30 minutes to an hour for the wilted vegetables to perk up.

## PERFECT POACHED EGGS

*A*dding a bit of lemon juice to the water in which you poach eggs will help to keep them from breaking apart while cooking and also keep them firm and very white. Just add a few drops of lemon juice to the poaching water before bringing it to a simmer. Make sure the water is simmering gently before adding the eggs.

## PREVENTING PEELED APPLES FROM BROWNING

*A*pples are among the quickest fruits to turn brown after cutting, but lemons can help them to look and taste fresher long after they have been cut. As you pare them, place the apples into a pan of cold water containing a few drops of lemon juice. If you are planning on eating only half an apple, quickly rub a wedge of lemon or a small amount of lemon juice over the portion you intend to save for later.

## PREVENTING CELERY FROM TURNING BROWN

*T*he bright green color of fresh celery can be preserved with the addition of a little bit of lemon juice. To prevent celery from turning brown, soak it in cold water with lemon juice (one teaspoon of lemon juice per quart of water) before refrigerating. To crisp it up after it has been in the refrigerator for a while, follow the same steps before serving.

## REMOVING FISH ODORS FROM HANDS

*L*emon not only adds a marvelous flavor to fish and other types of seafood, but also really helps to eliminate fishy odors from the cook's hands after handling seafood. After preparing your favorite fish dish, just rub your hands with a piece of lemon dipped in table salt, then rinse with water. Your hands will not only smell better but will be much cleaner as a result.

## SMOOTH FROSTING

*I*f your baking recipe calls for a frosting that requires cooking, you'll find that it is sometimes difficult to keep the frosting from becoming granulated. You can use lemon juice to prevent this from happening by stirring $1/4$ to $1/2$ teaspoon lemon juice into the frosting you would use on a normal cake.

## PERKING UP WILTED LETTUCE

*L*ettuce is a vegetable that can really be "brought back from the dead" by using a little bit of lemon juice and some cool water. Add a teaspoon of lemon juice to a bowl of cold water and soak the lettuce for a 30 minutes to an hour in the refrigerator.

## SOUR CREAM SUBSTITUTE

*I*f you can't get to the grocery store to buy some sour cream, but you have some lemon juice and whipping cream at home, you'll be surprised to see how well the combination of these two items works as a substitute for sour cream. Simply add 3 to 4 drops of pure lemon juice to every $^3/_4$ cup of whipping cream, and then let the mixture sit at room temperature for 30 to 40 minutes.

## STEWING TENDER CHICKENS

*L*emon not only adds a great flavor to chicken and other types of poultry, but it can also help to tenderize these birds while cooking. If you're planning to stew chicken or other types of poultry, just add a quartered lemon to the pot before stewing.

## TENDERIZING FISH

*F*or great seafood cooking, marinate your fish in $^1/_4$ cup lemon juice for every pound of fish for 20 minutes before cooking. This will make the fish tender, prevent it from drying out, and add a great flavor to your favorite fish dishes.

*California produces nearly one-third of all the lemons in the world.*

## TENDERIZING MEAT

*L*emon is a natural meat tenderizer. Before cooking meat, marinate it in lemon juice for several hours in the refrigerator. Use ¹/₄ cup lemon juice per pound of meat in the marinade.

## THINNER ICING

*I*f you are finishing off a cake with icing and find that it is becoming too thick, you can use lemon juice to thin out the icing and improve the texture and consistency of the icing. Just add a few lemon drops at a time to the icing and continue mixing until you reach the desired thickness and consistency.

## WHIPPING CREAM

*I*f your electric mixer is out of order and you need to make whipped cream the old-fashioned way, lemon juice can make the task much more manageable by reducing the time it takes to whip heavy cream. Just add 6 to 8 drops of lemon juice to each pint of heavy cream. This will yield approximately two cups of whipped cream.

## WHIPPING CREAM SUBSTITUTE

*E*vaporated milk can be used in place of whipping cream if you first place the can in the freezer until almost frozen, then pour it into a precooled bowl and add 1 tablespoon of lemon juice and ⅔ cup of milk. This combination will whip up very nicely—and also cut a few calories from the recipe.

## WOODEN WARE ODORS

*W*ooden bowls, spoons, salad utensils, and chopping boards have a tendency to pick up and hold odors from such pungent foods as garlic and onions. Get rid of the odors on these wooden kitchen products by rubbing the surface with the cut side of a lemon. Let it dry before washing as usual.

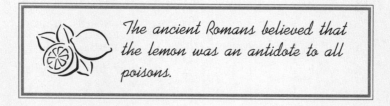

*The ancient Romans believed that the lemon was an antidote to all poisons.*

# In the Laundry

## BERRY STAINS ON WASHABLE CLOTHING

*D*ark berry stains can often mean the end of your favorite blouse or other item of clothing. As soon as possible after staining, sponge with lemon juice or rub a freshly cut lemon into the stain. Rinse with water, blot out all the moisture you can, and let it air-dry the rest of the way. If the stain remains, add a few drops of vinegar to a damp sponge and tamp while sponging if the fabric will tolerate it. Apply a laundry pretreat solution and wash in warm water. If the stain remains, soak in detergent for 30 minutes to an hour and launder again.

## REMOVING INK STAINS

*L*emon juice in combination with cream of tartar can be used to successfully remove ink spots from fabric that has been stained by leaking pens. Put enough cream of tartar over the stain to cover it and then drizzle a few drops of lemon juice over the stain. Rub the mixture into the stain for a couple of minutes and then remove the powder with a clean brush and sponge immediately with warm water. Repeat these steps if needed.

## LINT REMOVER

*L*int can mar the appearance of freshly laundered clothing. To remedy this, add $1/4$ cup lemon juice to your wash cycle to prevent lint from sticking to your white or lightly colored clothes.

## PRETREAT LAUNDRY
## SOLUTION

*L*emon juice in combination with baking soda can form an effective yet safe and natural laundry pretreatment solution. Just mix together equal parts of lemon juice and baking soda to form a paste. Apply this paste to hard-to-get-out stains by rubbing it into the stained area before laundering as usual.

## MILD BLEACH

*I*f you want to avoid using harsh chemical bleaches but still need a little something extra in your laundry to get out tough stains, try using lemon juice in combination with baking soda. This combination will result in a safe, mild natural bleach that is suitable for use with delicate fabrics. Add $^{1}/_{4}$ cup lemon juice and $^{1}/_{4}$ cup baking soda to your wash cycle and launder as usual.

## MILDEW ON FABRICS

*I*f mildew has set on clothing or anything else made of fabric, lemon juice can help remedy the situation. Just saturate the mildewed area with lemon juice and then rub table salt on it. Afterward, put the item in the sun for several hours, then finish up by washing and drying as usual.

# RESTORING STAINED WHITE AND LIGHT-COLORED ITEMS

*S*pread the washed wet items flat on an old sheet on the grass or a picnic table. Leave them out all day. If stains remain on the items, wet the stains with lemon juice, turn the garments over on the other side, and leave out overnight to catch the dew.

## FABRIC WHITENER AND BLEACH SUBSTITUTE

*L*emon juice makes for a great bleach substitute that is completely safe, nontoxic, and smells great, too. Just add ¼ cup of lemon juice to the wash cycle and wash and rinse as usual. Finish up by allowing the laundered items to air-dry in the sun, and you'll find that the result will be brighter, fresher-smelling clothes.

## RUST STAINS

*R*ust stains can be a real disappointment to find in your laundry, but lemon juice can help to remove these hard-to-get-out stains. Cover the stained area with salt and squeeze lemon juice on the top. Let stand for one hour. Brush with a scrub brush and wash and dry as usual.

## SCORCH MARKS ON WASHABLE FABRICS

*I*f you've got scorch marks on clothing but the fabric is still intact, try using lemon juice to help bleach out the scorched stain. Just rub a cut lemon into the scorched part, leaving as much juice and pith (the white layer beneath the outer rind) as possible on the fabric. Place the material in the sun to dry, then wash and dry as usual.

## WHITEN DULL SOCKS

*T*o revitalize your dingy old socks, try using lemon juice to give them a bright new appearance. Boil a pot of water, add two slices of lemon or $1/2$ teaspoon lemon juice, and soak for 10 minutes, then wash as usual. Lemon juice is an old-fashioned yet effective and safe whitener and mild bleach. Its natural whitening properties can be enhanced if the item can then be air-dried in the sun.

# WHITENING ATHLETIC SHOES

*T*hose old white cloth, vinyl, or suede tennis shoes can be given a bright new appearance by using lemon juice. To bleach your white athletic shoes so that they become "ultra-white," add lemon juice to the final rinse if the shoes are being washed in the laundry. If they cannot be laundered, rub lemon juice onto the surface and air-dry in the sun until they are white again.

*"A Persian's heaven is easily made: 'Tis but black eyes and lemonade."*

—THOMAS MOORE, *Intercepted Letters*

# *In the Cleaning Closet*

## AIR FRESHENER

*A*ll sorts of unwanted odors can be minimized or even eliminated by using the natural freshness of lemons to improve the air quality in your home or office. To create your own homemade air freshener with lemons, boil one or two cut-up lemons in two or three cups of water and pour the liquid into bowls throughout the house. Another way that lemons can freshen the air is to dissolve one teaspoon lemon juice and one teaspoon baking soda in two cups of hot water. Pour the mixture into a spray bottle and spray as you would any aerosol air freshener. This air freshener is completely free of chemicals, however, and is guaranteed not to damage the environment or the ozone.

## ALL-PURPOSE CLEANER

*T*his is a really effective, cost-efficient, totally natural cleaner that can be used for all sorts of everyday household cleaning tasks. It can be made by combining 2 tablespoons lemon juice, 1 teaspoon borax, $\frac{1}{2}$ teaspoon washing soda, $\frac{1}{4}$ to $\frac{1}{2}$ teaspoon liquid soap, and 2 cups very hot tap water in a spray bottle. Gently shake the mixture until all of the ingredients are dissolved, then apply to soiled or greasy surfaces in your kitchen, bathroom, or anywhere else around your house that you would use a conventional spray cleaner.

## COPPER CLEANER

*T*he original shiny luster can be restored to copper by removing the green tarnish that occurs when copper oxidizes. Cut a lemon in half and sprinkle it with a little salt and then use it to rub over copper items to shine dulled surfaces. Rinse with water and dry with a soft cloth before buffing to restore the original shine.

## STAINLESS STEEL
## CLEANER

Water spots and other stains that dull the surface of stainless steel sinks can be removed by using half a lemon with a little salt sprinkled over it. Apply the lemon-salt combination to the sink and rub away the surface discoloration. Follow up by buffing until the original luster is restored. This treatment also works wonders on any other stainless steel items that need cleaning around your house or garage.

## BRASS CLEANER

Your favorite brass candleholders, fireplace implements, doorknobs, or handrails can be restored to their original brilliance by using lemons in combination with salt. Just dip the cut side of a lemon in salt and rub it on the brass surface. Follow by rinsing with cold water and buffing with a soft cloth. Finally, you may want to coat your shiny new surface with silicone car wax to keep it shiny.

## CHROME CLEANER

*I*f your vintage automobile, bicycle, or anything else that has a lot of chrome on it is in need of a little shining, try using lemon to restore the metal alloy to its original brilliance. Rub the chrome items with the rind of a lemon, then rinse, dry, and buff until shiny.

## CRYSTAL CLEANER

*Y*our favorite heirloom crystal glassware can be safely cleaned by using lemon. You'll find that the water spots or other stains will wipe right off by gently rubbing the surface of a cut half lemon onto the crystal. Finish by rubbing with a damp, soft cloth and carefully drying the crystal with another soft cloth.

## VASE CLEANER

*V*ases that are made from either glass or ceramic material that are stained in the interior portion of the vase can be cleaned by using this combination of lemon juice, black tea, and water.

Take two cups of hot water and add two tea bags and allow the tea to steep until it is good and strong. Then let the tea cool and add $1/2$ cup lemon juice to the tea and pour the mixture into the vase. Allow the liquid to sit in the vase for a couple of hours, then scrub with a bottle brush, rinse, and dry.

## DRAIN CLEANER

*T*he drain in your sink or bathroom can benefit from an extra lemon cleaning from time to time. Measure out $1/2$ cup lemon juice and $1/2$ cup baking soda. Pour the baking soda into the drain first and follow with the lemon juice. The chemical interaction between baking soda and lemon juice will make a lot of noise, so be prepared. Leave the mixture for 15 minutes before rinsing with hot tap water.

## ALUMINUM CLEANER

*A*luminum, a metal once valued more than gold, can also benefit from lemons when it has lost its luster. To shine dull aluminum, rub the clouded aluminum surface with the cut side of a lemon until shiny again.

## FURNITURE POLISH

*T*his homemade furniture polish is easy to make and really brings out the natural beauty of the wood grain in your wooden furniture pieces at home. Make the polish by mixing two parts olive oil with one part lemon juice. Then, apply the mixture to furniture with a soft cloth, rubbing it into the wood. Finish off by wiping and buffing the wood until dry.

## GLASS CLEANER

*A* little lemon juice can make for a great natural window and glass cleaner. Just rub a small quantity of lemon juice over the glass surface, dry with paper towels, and shine with newspaper for sparkling glass.

## CLEANING WOOD PANELING AND CABINETS

*T*his is a great formula for cleaning greasy or dirty wood cabinets or paneling. It comes in handy during spring cleaning at your summer cottage, or anywhere else that has old woodwork in

need of a thorough cleaning. You can make the for-
mula by mixing $\frac{1}{4}$ cup lemon juice, $\frac{1}{8}$ cup linseed
oil, and $\frac{1}{8}$ cup vinegar in a glass jar. Rub into the
wood with a soft cloth until clean and finish by drying and buffing.

## ODOR-FREE
## HUMIDIFIERS

*T*he home humidifier can become ridden with
unwanted bacteria and as a result the mist
becomes smelly and unhealthy. A great way to eliminate odors that come from the unwanted bacteria in
home humidifiers is to pour 3 to 4 capfuls of bottled
lemon juice in the water and then run your humidifier as usual.

## IVORY CLEANER

*O*ld piano keys, carvings, or anything else that
is made of ivory can be cleaned by using salt.
When ivory begins to yellow, treat it with this
lemon-salt mixture. Cut a lemon in half, dip it in salt,
and rub it over the ivory surface. Let the surface dry,
wipe it with a damp cloth, and buff it dry for a

brighter finish. Another way to clean ivory is simply to rub the surface with a soft cloth moistened with lemon juice and then rinse with a clean cloth wrung out in clean water. Finish up by drying with another soft, clean cloth.

## LEATHER CLEANER

*L*eather goods such as shoes, jackets, saddles, and furniture can benefit from a lemon cleaning once in awhile. Take a lemon and slice it in half. Then, holding on to the rind, rub the leather with the lemon until it is fresh and clean.

## HAND CLEANER FOR
## AUTO WORK

*T*hose who like to work under the hood of a car can find that cleanup is much easier if they first rub a bit of lemon juice onto their hands before washing. Simply take a cut lemon and rub into the greasy areas of your hands before washing. For hard-to-get dirt under the fingernails, try soaking your fingers in lemon juice for 15 minutes to get rid of all the grease both on and underneath your nails.

## REMOVING MARBLE
## TABLETOP STAINS

*M*arble can be really difficult to clean due to its porous nature; it really absorbs dirt and other materials that come in contact with it. But lemon and a bit of salt can help clean marble without damaging its delicate surface. Sprinkle salt on a freshly cut lemon. Rub very lightly over the stain, being certain not to rub too hard or you will ruin the polished surface. Follow by washing with a mild soap and water.

## RESTORING SCUFFED LUGGAGE

*I*f the baggage handlers have really let loose with your expensive luggage, resulting in unsightly black marks, try using lemon to restore the luggage to its original condition. Use a small quantity of lemon extract and rub it into the scuffed area until the marks are gone.

## TAR CLEANER

*I*f your kids come home from a hot summer day of playing outdoors and their clothes have been stained by tar or asphalt, don't despair. Just mix a solution of equal parts lemon juice and linseed oil, wet a cloth with the mixture, and rub it on the clothing until the tar lifts off the surface.

## VACUUM CLEANER FRESHENER

*T*he dirt and other unwanted items vacuumed off your carpet or wood or tiled floor can result in a musty, unfresh odor emanating from the vacuum cleaner. A great way to remedy this is to put a cotton ball moistened with lemon juice in your vacuum bag each time you change the bag.

## WOOD FLOOR SOAP

*I*f you want to customize the scent of your floor cleaner and make a mixture that will really do a good job on floors, try mixing this combination in your mop bucket at home. In the bucket combine $1/2$ cup lemon juice, $1/8$ cup liquid soap, $1/2$ cup fragrant herbal tea, and 2 gallons of warm water. Stir until the mixture becomes sudsy and mop away.

## WOOD FURNITURE CLEANER AND POLISHER

*T*his is a great, economical substitute for the chemical-laden, lemon-scented commercial wood cleaners and furniture polishes, which are so widely used. Mix ¼ cup lemon juice, ⅛ cup vinegar, and ⅛ cup food-grade linseed oil in a glass jar. Then, using a soft cloth, rub into the wood until it is clean and finish off by wiping and buffing until dry. The rich nutty smell of the linseed oil is balanced by the light smell of lemon. To preserve this precious mixture, add a few drops of vitamin E, cover, and save the remaining portion for use at a later date.

## WOOD FURNITURE DUSTING AND CLEANING CLOTH

*Y*ou can make your own dusting and cleaning cloth that will pick up surface dust, clean, and leave a fresh lemon scent in the rooms that are dusted. To make the solution, mix ¼ cup lemon juice and ½ teaspoon olive oil in a small bowl. Then dab a soft cotton rag or chamois cloth into the solution and dust, clean, and shine your wooden furniture with it. You can reuse the cloth over and over again.

# *In the Bathroom*

## REMOVING TOILET BOWL RINGS

*L*emon combined with readily available borax can make an efficient and fresh-smelling toilet bowl cleaner. To make the cleaning solution, start by placing some powdered borax in a small bowl. Add enough lemon juice to the borax to get a nice thick paste and then let the paste sit for about 2 hours. To remove toilet bowl rings, flush first to wet the sides of the bowl and apply the borax and lemon juice paste to the stained area. Let the paste sit on the sides of the toilet bowl for about 20 minutes and finish up by scrubbing with a toilet brush until clean.

## CLEANING SHOWER DOOR TRACKS

*T*he hard-to-clean space that is found inside a shower door track can become very mildewed and dirty. If you mix together the juice of half a lemon, one tablespoon of bleach, and a cup of water and pour it into a spray bottle, you'll have a powerful cleaning and germ-killing solution that will really work on mildewy areas like shower door tracks. Once you've mixed the solution, spray it on the mildewed area, being careful not to inhale the mist. Then, let the solution stand for a couple of minutes and finally rinse with warm water.

## REMOVING RUST STAINS ON PORCELAIN TUBS AND SINKS

*R*ust stains from old cast-iron faucets or rusty pipes can really mire the beauty of a genuine porcelain bathtub or wash basin. If the porcelain surface is lightly stained, try rubbing it with a cut lemon until the stain disappears. If it is a deeper stain, make a thick paste of borax and lemon juice, and rub on the rust stains. Repeat, if necessary, until the stain is gone and the porcelain is again clean and white.

## REMOVING FAUCET MINERAL DEPOSITS

*T*his mixture will clear the water spots and mineral residues from metal bathroom or kitchen faucets. Dissolve 1 teaspoon alum in ¼ cup lemon juice. Soak a cloth in the mixture and leave it on the area for a few hours before rinsing. (Alum can be obtained from a drugstore or the spice section of a supermarket.)

## OLD MIRROR RESTORER

*L*emon can be used to restore old, cloudy mirror surfaces to their shiny original condition. Apply a thin coat of reconstituted lemon juice to the stained portion of the mirror, and then rub until the stain is gone and the mirror is dry.

*Much of the lemon in household products isn't lemon at all but a combination of chemicals that smells like lemon.*

# REMOVING SHOWER CURTAIN MOLD

*S*hower curtains are one of the hardest household items to keep free of mold and mildew, but lemon and borax combined can make even the moldiest shower curtain clean and fresh again. Combine ⅓ cup lemon juice and ⅓ cup borax to make a paste, and scrub this paste on the shower curtain using a sponge; follow up by rinsing well. To make the job easier, remove the curtain and put it in the bathtub, or have someone pull on the bottom of the curtain to make it taut while you scrub on the paste. Then, if possible, let the curtain hang to dry outdoors in the sun.

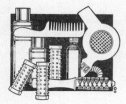

# *For Beauty*

## AGE SPOTS

*T*he appearance of these spots—resembling an early form of cancer to the untrained eye—can be scary. But genuine age spots (sometimes known as liver spots) are really nothing more than adult freckles resulting from overexposure to the sun. They actually have nothing to do with the liver, and little to do with age, except that they generally occur on older people. The juice of a fresh lemon is acidic enough to safely peel off the upper layer of skin and will remove or lighten some age spots. Rub lemon juice on the age spots with a cotton ball twice daily, and in 6 to 8 weeks they should begin to fade away.

## BLACKHEAD REMEDY

*B*efore going to bed, rub lemon juice over blackheads. Wait until morning to wash off the juice with cool water. Repeat this procedure several evenings in a row and you'll see a big improvement in your skin.

## CALLUS REMOVER

*F*or calloused hands, feet, or any other roughened areas of the skin, try using a bit of lemon juice to restore the skin's softness. Just put a thin slice of lemon directly on the calloused area and secure it with a Band-Aid. Leave lemon on overnight. Lemon juice works to soften the callus because it is a weak acid and helps break down the thickened dead skin that forms the callus.

## CHAPPED HANDS CURE

*R*ed, rough, and sore hands can be relieved with lemon juice. Use a generous amount of lemon juice and massage it into your hands. Follow by rinsing off the lemon juice and massaging the hands with olive oil, coconut oil, or wheat germ oil.

## DANDRUFF RELIEF

*I*f you suffer from dandruff, try using lemon juice as a natural scalp restorative. To get rid of the dandruff, squeeze the juice of one large lemon and apply half of it to your hair. Mix the other half with 2 cups of water. Wash your hair with a mild shampoo, then rinse with water. Rinse again with the lemon and water mixture. Repeat every other day until dandruff disappears.

## FIGHTING FACIAL BLEMISHES

*L*emon juice works as an all-natural acne fighter. It can help restore the skin and overcome this troublesome condition without having to resort to expensive chemical preparations. Apply lemon juice to the skin with a cotton pad by lightly dabbing the affected area a few times a day until the blemish disappears. The acidity in the lemon will help your

*The ladies of Louis XIV's court made a habit of occasionally biting lemons in order to keep their lips seductively red.*

skin to rid itself of pimples and other blemishes that mar the surface.

## FACIAL CLEANSER

*F*or a deep cleanse, try this lemony concoction. Bring 1 quart of water to a boil and take it to the table or rest the pot in the kitchen or bathroom sink. Add the juice or peel of half a lemon and a handful of herbs—rosemary, basil, thyme, mint, whatever. Then cover your hair with a shower cap and drape a towel over your head and the pot while keeping your face about 12 inches from the water. Close your eyes and let your face steam for 15 minutes. Rinse with clear, cold water to close your pores. (NOTE: Don't use this method more than once a week or you may deplete your skin of too many natural oils.)

## HAIR CONDITIONER

*B*ound to draw raves, this hair conditioner will add new life and luster to dull and damaged hair. Combine ³/₄ cup olive oil, ¹/₂ cup honey, the juice of one lemon, and set aside. Rinse your hair with water and towel-dry. Work in a small amount of the conditioner (store what's left over in the refrigerator) and comb through to distribute the mixture evenly. Then cover with a plastic bag or plastic for $1/2$ hour. Follow up by shampooing and rinsing thoroughly.

## HEALING CHLORINE-DAMAGED HAIR

*I*f pool chlorine is turning your blond hair green, after swimming you can help your hair with a solution of lemon juice and baking soda. When you leave the pool, thoroughly wash and rinse your hair. Then mix $1/2$ cup baking soda with the juice of one lemon; this mixture will bubble up after mixing and should be promptly massaged into your hair. Follow up by a second thorough rinsing and drying.

## HIGHLIGHTING BLOND HAIR

*L*emon juice can act as a kind of natural peroxide for those of us who want to lighten our hair color without having to resort to the hair color bottle. Rinse your hair with $1/4$ cup lemon juice diluted with $3/4$ cups water. Follow up by sitting in the sun or exercising outdoors on a warm, sunny day until the desired level of highlights comes out in your hair.

## NONTOXIC HAIR SPRAY

*M*any people have allergic reactions to hair spray, which can easily end up on delicate facial skin instead of on the hair. Eye and nasal irritations are common side effects from toxic hair spray as well. You can make your own hair spray from lemons and avoid all of the toxic dangers of store-bought brands. Chop one lemon. Place it in a pot and cover with 2 cups of hot water. Boil the mixture until only half of the water remains. Cook and strain. Place in a spray bottle and test on hair. If it's too sticky, add more water. Store in the refrigerator or add 1 ounce of vodka per cup of hair spray as a preservative. (With the vodka, you can keep the hair spray unrefrigerated for up to two weeks.)

## TAMING HAIR STATIC

*L*emon juice can help tame the hair static that occurs during dry times of the year. For flyaway hair, mix ½ teaspoon lemon juice and ¼ teaspoon lime juice with ½ cup of water in a spray bottle. Shake to mix. Spray on your hair to tame static. Store the remaining mixture in the refrigerator.

## LOW-COST MANICURE

*F*or a low-cost manicure, soak your fingertips in a mixture of 1 cup lukewarm water and the juice of $1/2$ lemon for about 5 minutes. Rinse and pat dry, pushing the cuticles back as you dry. Then rub a lemon peel over your nails and finish up by buffing with a soft cloth.

## MOISTURIZING DRY SKIN

*T*he juice of lemons combined with baby oil can work wonders as a skin moisturizer. The fragrant oil will enter your skin and provide lubrication to thirsty cells and tissues. Like sponges, the pores will absorb the lemon oil and be invigorated. To make the solution, add 1 tablespoon of lemon juice to $1/2$ cup of baby oil. Begin by soaking in a warm bath for 10 minutes to steam open your pores. Then get out of the tub and gently massage the lemon oil into the skin. This mixture works well both as a facial and body moisturizer, so be sure to use it all over your body.

## NAIL CLEANER

*I*f you have stubborn grease or dirt underneath your fingernails, try using half a lemon as a nail cleaner. Insert your fingertips in half a lemon and twist your fingers back and forth to clean your cuticles and nails. This method also works well as a premanicure cleansing technique.

## NAIL WHITENER

*L*emon juice is the natural and safe way to whiten and brighten nails. Just soak your nails in lemon juice for 5 to 10 minutes, then brush them with a mixture of equal parts white vinegar and warm water. Follow by rinsing well with clean water.

## HAND REVITALIZER

*Y*ou can use lemon juice in combination with other natural ingredients to revitalize your hands. To make a great hand cream, mix together 1 tablespoon lemon juice, 1 tablespoon honey, and 1 cup oatmeal. Stir together in a bowl until they form a moist paste. Work the paste into clean hands and cover with cotton gloves for 20 minutes. Rinse and follow up with moisturizer (see above for a home-made skin moisturizer).

## PLAQUE AND TARTAR REMOVER

*O*ral hygiene can be vastly improved with the addition of occasional lemon treatments to the teeth and gums. For this treatment, swish 1 or 2 tablespoons of lemon juice around in your mouth so that it mixes with your saliva, then swallow slowly. Next, take a lemon rind and rub your teeth and mas-sage your gums with it. The upper gums should be massaged downward; the lower gums should be massaged upward. The results are fantastic for the teeth, gums—and your breath, too. (NOTE: Lemon juice is a strong acid and if used alone too often may damage tooth enamel. Lemon juice should be used with caution and only on an occasional basis in any cleaning solution for the teeth.)

## RESTORING ROUGH, DISCOLORED FEET

*L*emon can work well to restore your much-used feet. If your toes or the skin on your feet are discolored and rough, rub the affected areas with half a lemon. For extra bleaching and softening, cup the lemon on your heels for 15 minutes. Be sure to moisturize afterward.

## REMOVING DEAD SKIN CELLS

*P*atches of rough, dry skin can be successfully revitalized by using this combination of lemon and salt. Make a paste by combining $1/4$ cup of salt with approximately 2 teaspoons of lemon juice. Rub this abrasive mixture on any area of your body where the skin needs refreshing. Then wash off the paste—and the dead skin cells—with cool water.

## SOFTENING ROUGH ELBOWS AND KNEES

*U*se lemon juice to bleach and soften roughened elbows and knees. Place a few drops of baby oil on two lemon halves. Place the lemon halves over your knees or elbows and then tape the lemon halves in place and leave them on the affected areas for 30 minutes. Follow up by rinsing with cool water and then moisturizing.

## TOOTH WHITENER

*T*he natural whitening power of lemon juice can be utilized for a whiter, brighter smile. For an occasional whitener of your teeth, mix together 1 teaspoon baking soda and ½ teaspoon lemon juice. Apply a coat of this paste to your teeth, using a cotton swab. Brush clean with water, then rinse. Coffee and tea stains will disappear. (NOTE: Lemon juice is a strong acid and if used alone too often may damage tooth enamel. Lemon juice should be used with caution and only on an occasional basis in any cleaning solution for the teeth.)

## WRINKLE REMEDY

*A*s a means of rejuvenating the skin, lemon juice can prove most effective. This wrinkle preventative is an ancient formula known to be used by the women of France. To make the solution, boil 1 cup milk, 2 teaspoons lemon juice, and 1 tablespoon brandy. While the mixture is warm, paint it on the face and neck with a pastry brush. When thoroughly dry, wash it off with warm water and pat dry. Follow up by moisturizing.

# *For Health*

## RELIEVING ACHING FEET

*A*t the end of a hard day, try a refreshing foot-bath followed by a lemon treatment to relieve sore feet. Begin by soaking achy feet in hot water for 10 to 15 minutes. If you like, add Epsom or other mineral salts to the footbath. Then follow up by massaging your feet with ample amounts of lemon juice. This will make your feet feel and smell much better and also improve the condition of the skin of your feet. After a thorough massage, rinse your feet with cool, refreshing water. As always, dry feet completely afterward, then apply your favorite moisturizer and spend some time relaxing and enjoying how good your feet feel.

## ATHLETE'S FOOT REMEDY

*L*emon's inherent sanitizing properties can be used as a natural cure for athlete's foot. After washing and gently drying the feet, rub generous amounts of lemon juice onto the affected areas. This solution may be of help to some sufferers of athlete's foot or other fungal infections. A word of caution, however: If the feet are particularly raw or cracked, the lemon juice can cause stinging when applied to the feet.

## BAD BREATH CURE

*T*he freshness of lemons can be an aid to those who suffer from bad breath. To alleviate halitosis, add a couple of teaspoons of lemon juice to water and drink up for fresher, better-smelling breath.

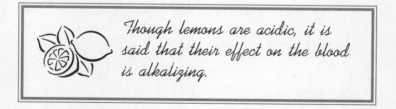

*Though lemons are acidic, it is said that their effect on the blood is alkalizing.*

## CURING BLADDER INFECTIONS

*F*resh lemon juice in water is an excellent curative for bladder infections. Add a couple of teaspoons to each glass of water you drink while recuperating from a bladder infection. Remember to drink plenty of water to flush out the infection and to return to good health again.

## KIDNEY STONE PREVENTION

*T*he magnesium and citric acid that can be found in lemon juice are two key ingredients in the prevention of the most common forms of kidney stones—those that are chiefly composed of calcium oxalate. To both prevent and cure kidney stones, make lemon juice a daily addition to your drinking water. Add 1 teaspoon of lemon juice to a glass of drinking water on a regular basis.

## HEALING BLEEDING CUTS

*I*f you have a minor wound with bleeding that is not too severe, you can use lemon to help the body's natural ability to heal itself. Just squeeze a few drops of juice directly on the cut before bandaging. Lemon works as an effective disinfectant and also helps the body to stop the wound from bleeding. You should first brace yourself, however, for the sting.

## BOIL REDUCER

*I*f you are suffering from a minor boil, you can use a lemon to speed the healing and alleviate the pain from a boil. Begin by heating a lemon in the oven until it is hot, though not too hot to place on the skin. Set the oven to a warming temperature (about 150 degrees Fahrenheit) and heat the lemon for about 10 minutes. Then slice it in half and place a half on your boil. Secure it in place for about 1 hour.

## RELIEVING BRONCHITIS

*I*f you are suffering from bronchitis or any other chest condition that results in a cough, lemon juice with ginger can help relieve these conditions. Just add 2 teaspoons of lemon juice and $1/2$ teaspoon of fresh grated ginger to 1 cup hot water and drink the fluid slowly. This can help to alleviate throat tickling, which can provoke coughing, and it

also works to expedite the movement of mucus from the bronchial tubes and the chest.

## CONSTIPATION REMEDY

*I*f irregularity is a problem, try using lemon juice and water to stimulate the digestive system and alleviate mild constipation. Drinking water on an empty stomach can stimulate peristalsis (the movement of the intestines), and if you add lemon juice to the water, you'll find that it will further stimulate the intestines. Before breakfast, drink the juice of ½ lemon in 1 cup of warm water. In addition to aiding the digestive system, it should also help to cleanse your body of toxins. If you find the sourness of lemon a bit much so early in the day, try sweetening the mixture with honey.

## REMOVING CORNS

*C*orns can be a troublesome and painful occurrence on feet, and lemons can really help to remove these pesky skin growths. To remove corns, apply one piece of fresh lemon peel on the corn (the inside of the peel on the corn) every night before bed. Place a Band-Aid around the lemon peel to keep it in place. In a few days, the corn should be gone.

## COUGH REMEDY FOR CHILDREN

*I*f you are looking for an old-fashioned, natural yet effective cure for your children's cough, try using this formula to alleviate your little one's coughing. Combine the juice of ½ lemon with 1 tablespoon honey, and stir in ½ teaspoon butter to make the mixture a lubricating consistency. Coat the back of your child's throat with the mixture to relieve the coughing.

## COUGH SYRUPS

*L*emon can be a key ingredient in homemade cough syrups that do not contain alcohol, codeine, or any other unwanted chemical additives. You'll find that your children are much less likely to complain about the taste with homemade cough syrups with lemon added, and that they work just as well as the more expensive store-bought products. Below are two recipes for cough syrup formulas that you can try:

1. For 5 minutes, cook the juice of 1 lemon, 1 cup of honey, and $^1/_2$ cup olive oil. Then stir vigorously for a couple of minutes. Take 1 teaspoonful every two hours.

2. For a more delicious, thirst-quenching, and soothing drink, squeeze the juice of 1 lemon into a big mug or glass. Add hot water, 2 tablespoons of honey, and either 3 whole cloves or a $^1/_2$-inch piece of stick cinnamon. Drink one glass of this mixture every 3 hours.

## EYEWASH

*I*f your eyes are in need of a little help, you can use lemon juice and water to reinvigorate them. To make a soothing solution, mix 1 drop of lemon juice in 1 ounce of warm water and use it as an eyewash. It's particularly effective when your eyes have been exposed to dust, cigarette smoke, harsh lights, and chemical compounds in the air.

*Lemons are not only rich in vitamin C but also in calcium, potassium, and magnesium.*

## FEVER REDUCER

*T*his is an old medicinal recipe that is said to help the body to fight a fever. Mix 2 to 3 tablespoons lemon juice, $^1/_2$ teaspoon cod liver oil, and honey to taste. Take 1 teaspoon of this mixture when you feel a fever coming on.

## HEALING HANGNAILS

*H*angnails can be a real nuisance. When you have one of these painful inflammations around the finger or toe, soak the affected area in hot water. Then heat a lemon in the oven, cut a narrow opening in the middle, and sprinkle salt in it. Take the infected finger or toe and stick it in the lemon. Within minutes, the pain should disappear, and you'll find that the skin surrounding the hangnail will heal much more quickly.

## ENDING HEARTBURN

*A*cid indigestion as a result of eating too many sweets can be alleviated by using a combination of lemon juice and salt. If you find yourself experiencing heartburn from eating something sweet, squeeze $1/2$ lemon into 1 cup of warm water. Add $1/2$ teaspoonful of salt and drink slowly.

## HICCUP STOPPER

*I*t is said that sucking on a lemon wedge can work as an immediate cure for some sufferers of hiccups. As soon as the annoying hiccups start, cut a lemon wedge or two and begin sucking until the hiccups stop. The combination of the sourness and the sucking should bring your diaphragm back to normal in no time at all.

## LARYNGITIS/HOARSENESS REMEDY

*T*alking too much, smoking too much, or being in a dusty, dry environment can lead to occasional laryngitis or hoarseness of the throat area. To make a great natural throat restorative, beat the white of an organic egg for 2 minutes, then add 1 teaspoon of lemon juice and 1 teaspoon of honey. Mix well. Drink the mixture in the morning and in the evening, gargling for a bit before swallowing until the condition is remedied.

# INSECT BITE RELIEF

*I*f you are suffering from redness, swelling, and itching from pesky insect bites, try using lemon juice to help the skin heal itself. Simply dab lemon juice directly on the bites that have come from mosquitoes, fleas, flies, or any other insect. Lemon juice acts quickly to heal the pain, alleviate the itching, and act as a natural anti-inflammatory remedy for any insect bite that is troubling you.

# MOTION SICKNESS PREVENTATIVE

*A*n old-time cure for seasickness can help out with this troublesome malady and any other type of motion sickness you might experience. If you are feeling queasy or are about to embark on an ocean journey, beat one organic egg white together with the juice of a lemon and swallow the mixture just before you take off on your trip. Or take immediately as you begin to feel the effects of motion sickness.

## PAINLESS PAPER CUTS

*A*s soon as you feel the sting of a paper cut, clean the cut with the juice of a lemon. Then, to ease the pain, wet the cut finger and dip it into powdered cloves. Since cloves act as a mild anesthetic, the pain should be gone in a matter of seconds and the cut should close itself and heal much more quickly as a result.

## POISON IVY AND POISON OAK REMEDY

*H*iking trips and other outdoor forays can be very enjoyable, but if you find yourself itching and irritated after one of these excursions from brushing against pain-causing poison ivy or poison oak, make sure to have a few lemons on hand to aid in healing. Slice 1 or 2 lemons and rub slices all over the affected areas. It should stop the itching and help clear up the skin. Repeat daily until the skin is free from irritation.

## PYORRHEA PREVENTATIVE

*C*ut the scrubbed rind of a lemon and massage the gums with the inside of the slices of rind. Not only may this treatment prevent pyorrhea, but it will also help remove stains from the teeth. (NOTE: Lemon juice is a strong acid and if used alone too often may damage tooth enamel. Lemon juice should be used with caution and only on an occasional basis in any cleaning solution for the teeth.)

## SOOTHING A SORE THROAT

*I*t is widely accepted that lemon is one of the very best substances for soothing the achiness of a sore throat. To make this effective home remedy, take the juice of a large lemon and mix it with 1 teaspoon of honey. Swallow a dose of this every 2 hours until your throat feels better. Another way to use lemon juice to remedy your sore throat is to make a hot lemon drink. Just add the juice from one lemon to a glass of hot water and sweeten to taste with about $1\frac{1}{2}$ teaspoons of honey. Drink a glass of this mixture every 4 hours.

## SUNBURN REMEDY

*A*n old Italian remedy for quickly taking the red out of a sunburn is to slice a lemon in half and rub the lemon over the sunburned area. Be aware that the acid from the lemon will initially sting like crazy. But the Italians swear it is worth the pain because the red will fade very quickly as a result.

# *In the Playroom*

## BOUNCING BALLS IN A BOWL

*I*f you're looking for new ways to amuse your kids, try this fun trick. You can make small items rise mysteriously in water and enjoy watching them sink again and float to the top. Start by filling a clear container with water (add food color for drama), $\frac{1}{4}$ cup lemon juice, and 3 tablespoons baking soda.

Then add lightweight items such as buttons or small uncooked pasta pieces and watch them bounce. Though the items will sink at first, they will begin to rise because the bubbles created by the lemon juice and baking soda reaction cling to them, lifting them to the surface. At the surface, the air bubbles break and they fall back to the bottom and the process begins anew. Renew the solution with three parts lemon juice to one part baking soda, as needed.

## INVISIBLE INK

You can write secret messages that can be read later at the discretion of the recipient. Write a message on a piece of paper with a cotton swab, using lemon juice as invisible ink. After the ink is dry, hold the paper near a hot lightbulb. The writing will turn brown and you'll be able to read the message.

## JUGGLING LEMONS

Lemons are just the right size and weight for a beginning or accomplished juggler. Take as many lemons as you can and toss them into the air, not allowing any to hit the floor.

# *Around the House*

## NO CATS ON FURNITURE

*T*o discourage your cat from jumping on your nice furniture or prowling in off-limit areas, touch the cat's lips very lightly with a cotton ball moistened with lemon juice. Each time the cat goes where it shouldn't be, leave a cotton ball moistened with lemon in that area.

## ENDING DOG BARKING

*F*or some nontoxic behavioral modification, try using a little lemon juice when training your dog. You can end your dog's annoying barking by squirting a little lemon juice in his mouth (not eyes) and saying "Quiet!" when he begins barking. You'll

find this to be a quick and harmless way of reform-
ing his behavior and giving yourself more peace.

## DRIED LEMON POTPOURRI

*T*he naturally fresh fragrance of lemons can be
captured and preserved by using this recipe
for your own homemade potpourri. Start by thinly
paring the outer rind of 6 large lemons. Put these on
a plate or in a bowl and rub in 1½ tablespoons of
orrisroot powder. Put the coated peels on nonstick
baking sheets and put them in a preheated oven at
300 degrees Fahrenheit. The rinds will take about
2½ to 3 hours to dry. They should be hard but not
brittle when you remove them from the oven. Cool
the rinds completely and store in airtight containers.
Just before use, coarsely crush or bruise the peels
with a pestle and mortar. You can place them
around the house or in your drawers to enjoy the
aroma of fresh lemon scent.

## FLEA CONTROL FOR DOGS

*I*f you want to help your dog to fight fleas but are
reluctant to dust him with awful-smelling flea
powder, try this lemon trick. Cut 4 lemons into

eighths and then cover with water and bring the lemons and water to a boil. Simmer the lemons and water on a low heat for about 45 minutes. Afterward, cool and strain the liquid and pour it into a glass container. Wet your animal thoroughly with the infusion, brushing his coat while wet so that the lemon juice and oil penetrate to the skin. Dry the fur thoroughly with a towel and then finish up by brushing again.

## HOMEMADE CITRUS POMANDERS FOR HOLIDAY DÉCOR

During the holiday season you can use the scent of lemons and other citrus fruits to really freshen up your home. Lemons, oranges, and grapefruits pierced with cloves exude a refreshing and tangy scent. Get several pieces of citrus fruit and pierce them in lines up and down the skin with cloves. If you tie some of the pieces of fruit with ribbons and add beads stuck on pins, you'll find that the fruit will look more festive. You can also arrange the fruit in a bowl as a centerpiece for your holiday table, and complete the display with a few pieces of fruit to eat. Your table will both look and smell wonderful.

## KEEPING ANTS OUT OF THE HOUSE

*P*eople love lemons, but fortunately ants don't! You can use lemons as a nontoxic pest-control substance to keep ants out of your house. Just squirt lemon juice on window sills and the bottoms of doors to keep ants from coming into the house. The ants will not cross the barrier.

## FIREPLACE DEODORIZER

*I*f you enjoy a warm fire on a cold winter day but don't like your house to become too smoky, try using a little lemon peel to freshen the fireplace. Add a lemon peel to the fire while it is burning and it will work well to prevent fireplace odors. You can also toss some peels on the smoldering coals once you've finished enjoying the fire, and it will make the room smell nice and fresh as a result.

## TREATING DOG MANGE

*I*f you find that your dog is suffering from the dreaded skin disorder mange and want to try using a natural cure before resorting to the vet, you can use lemons and garlic to ward off this disease. Start by adding 1 thinly sliced lemon and 1 peeled and grated garlic clove to 2 cups boiling water, then cool the mixture to room temperature. Once cooled, pour it over the affected areas twice a day until the problem is resolved.

## WOOD LIGHTENER

Wood can become dark and dingy after awhile, but lemon can help to restore the natural look of the unfinished grain. Just saturate a sponge with lemon juice and then wash the wood until you find that the grain lightens up to the desired degree. There is no need to follow up by rinsing.

# Lemon Oil

While raw lemons and their juice can be used on their own for countless health remedies and household problems, as well as to solve many beauty problems, an entire second dimension of the wonders of lemons can be found in lemon oil. Lemon oil can polish your furniture and leather goods, and it can also wax your car. So, instead of relying exclusively on the juice and rinds of lemons, make your own lemon oil from a lemon or two and expand the possibilities even further.

To make your own lemon oil, crush or pulverize one or two lemons (skin and all) with a mortar and pestle, blender, or food processor. Put ground lemon in a glass jar and just barely cover with pure walnut oil or another cold-pressed oil of your choice. Let sit, stirring twice a day, in a warm place for a week. Strain the oil and dilute it with more oil if it is too strong. To preserve your lemon oil, squeeze an open vitamin-E capsule into the oil and you'll find that it will be much more long lasting.

## FURNITURE CLEANER

*T*his formula works well as a basic cleaner that can be used either as an everyday household formula or as a pre-polish or pre-waxing cleaner that will get your furniture readied for a new look. Add about $1/2$ teaspoon of lemon oil to $1/4$ cup vinegar and rub the mixture into the furniture surface with a soft cloth to wipe away any dirty residue or dust that is on your furniture.

## FURNITURE POLISH

*Y*ou can make a great, all-natural, nontoxic furniture polish by using lemon oil, vinegar, and linseed oil. Combine $1/4$ cup food-grade linseed oil, $1/4$ cup vinegar, and $1/2$ teaspoon of lemon oil in a small jar, and shake thoroughly. Then apply the polish with a soft cloth on furniture or any wood surface until you have reached the desired level of saturation, and buff until dry.

# WOOD FURNITURE WAX

*T*his homemade wax works wonders on tired, old, finished and unfinished wood surfaces that are in need of refurbishing. Take $1/2$ cup food-grade linseed oil, 1 tablespoon carnauba wax, which is available at craft stores and woodworking stores, 1 tablespoon beeswax, $1/4$ cup vinegar, and 1 teaspoon of lemon oil and put all of the ingredients into the top half of a double boiler set over water. Slowly heat ingredients until they melt together, and stir until well blended. Pour the hot mixture out of the pan into a wide glass jar and let it cool, until the wax has completely solidified. You'll find that the vinegar will sink to the bottom. Once the mixture has solidified, pop it out of the jar. This is now your custom wax. Apply the wax to clean furniture with a soft rag and rub it into the wood surface. Then take another soft rag and dip it into the residue vinegar in the jar (or vinegar from a different bottle) and rub, buff, and polish the wax to a high shine. You'll find that the vinegar will smooth the wax out well. If you want to have a really hard wax surface, use 2 tablespoons of carnauba wax in the mixture instead of one.

## SOFT WAX FOR FURNITURE

*F*or a wax that renders a higher gloss, make a softer, pastier version of the wax above. Put 1 tablespoon of carnauba wax and 1 cup of food-grade linseed oil into a saucepan. Heat the two ingredients over a low heat until the carnauba wax is melted, stirring continuously. Once the ingredients are mixed together, remove the pan from the heat and add to it 1 teaspoon of lemon oil, stirring once again. Allow the mixture to cool down and you'll have a wax that is a little softer than petroleum jelly.

## LEATHER POLISH

*L*emon oil in combination with olive oil makes an excellent polish that will add new life to your worn leather shoes, jackets, gloves, or furniture. Take ¼ cup of olive oil and add ½ teaspoon of lemon oil to it. Mix the oils together by shaking them in a glass jar. Thoroughly wet a soft cloth with the oil and apply it to your leather items, making certain to really rub it into the material. Finish up by buffing until you get the desired amount of sheen.

## FLOOR POLISH

*T*o make an effective, wonderful-smelling floor polish, take 1 cup of food-grade linseed oil and add ½ teaspoon lemon oil and place in a glass jar and shake until mixed together. Then thoroughly soak a soft cloth with the oil and rub it into the floor. Finish up by buffing and polishing.

## AUTOMOBILE WAX

*T*his is a great natural car wax that will both protect the finish of your precious vehicle and allow it to shine like new. Take 1 cup of food-grade linseed oil, 4 tablespoons of beeswax, ½ cup of vinegar, and 1 teaspoon of lemon oil and put all of these ingredients—except for the lemon oil—into a saucepan or double boiler. Slowly heat the mixture

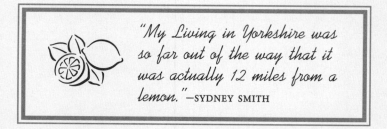

*"My Living in Yorkshire was so far out of the way that it was actually 12 miles from a lemon."* —SYDNEY SMITH

on a low flame or setting until all of the waxes are melted, stirring continuously. Once the waxes are blended, remove the pan from the heat and add the lemon oil and blend thoroughly. Pour the mixture into a jar or tin can and allow it to cool down. Once the wax has solidified, break it out of the container and rub it on the surface of your car. Then, soak a corner of a soft cloth with vinegar and buff and polish the wax to a high shine.

# A Taste of Lemon: Favorite Lemony Recipes

# Serving Suggestions

*L*emons serve both decorative and culinary pur-
poses. They can take an ordinary dish and give
it a nice extra burst of color and flavor. They are a
popular flavor enhancer and a good substitute for
salt. They add zest to soups, salads, and sauces,
cakes and ices, and are also used in the making of
marmalade.

## FANCY LEMON-WEDGE
## PRESENTATION

*F*or a restaurant-style presentation of a lemon
wedge to garnish a serving of fish or any other
dish nicely accented by a squeeze of lemon, set a
lemon half, cut side down, on a square of cheesecloth. Bring up the cheesecloth ends and tie them at
the top with a small ribbon or string. Place a
wrapped lemon half on each guest's plate. This presentation allows diners to squeeze out the juice

without worrying about seeds or chunks of flesh spurting onto their food.

## SALAD DRESSINGS

*L*emon juice makes a delicious alternative to bottled vinegar in homemade dressings. Any time that a dressing recipe calls for vinegar, try replacing the vinegar altogether or substituting part of it with lemon juice. You can do so by using twice as much lemon juice as vinegar in all or part of the recipe.

## SOUP AND STEW ENHANCER

*T*o enliven chicken broth, tomato soup, clam chowder, or beef stew, add a little lemon juice just before serving. Its fresh flavor will complement most spices and seasonings and add a pleasant extra taste to all sorts of soups and stews.

## FRUIT ENHANCER

*L*emon juice and zest can really improve the flavor and freshness of mixed fruit salads, cranberry sauce, applesauce, melons, and berries. Just add a squeeze of lemon or a small amount of zest to fresh or preserved fruit before serving. You'll find that it will also help to keep the color and texture of the fruit or preserves much fresher for a longer period.

## SEAFOOD GARNISH

*L*emons not only enhance the texture and flavor of fresh seafood but also make a most attractive table presentation for the main platter or individual plates of seafood. Garnish your fish or shellfish dish with slices of lemon by cutting the lemon thinly in round slices and ringing the plate with them or simply add a few cut lemon wedges to the outer portion of the plate.

*Lemons fall into three categories: common or acid lemons, which are the commercial varieties we all know; rough lemons, used chiefly as rootstock for other citrus fruits; and sweet lemons, which are horticultural curiosities.*

## LOW-FAT VEGETABLE ENHANCER

*A* great way to add flavor to cooked vegetable dishes without adding extra fat and calories is to sprinkle cooked green vegetables with lemon juice. You can also try mixing lemon juice with vegetable or chicken broth to use as a low-fat sauce. Just add 1 teaspoon of lemon juice to $^1/_4$ cup of broth for a great-tasting healthy sauce.

## DIP ENHANCER

*T*o give your yogurt or sour cream vegetable and chip dips a little extra burst of freshness, try stirring a small amount of lemon zest and herbs into the yogurt or sour cream. For a savory dip, add about $^1/_4$ teaspoon of zest to each $^1/_2$ cup of dip, and add fresh herbs to taste.

## FRUIT JUICE ACCENT

*A*lthough lemon juice requires considerable sweetening when served on its own as a beverage, it adds a delicious accent to other juices, such as orange, pineapple, or tomato. Just add a small amount of juice to taste to your favorite fruit juice for a little extra flavor.

## SALT SUBSTITUTE

*L*emon juice is a good flavoring to use in place of salt. For those with high blood pressure and others who need to cut down on salt intake, the tart refreshing juice from lemons can help you cut down by stimulating the taste buds in the same way that salt does. It also enhances the flavor of foods, such as rice, potatoes, salads, and cooked vegetables, while adding no fat and negligible calories. The acid contained in the juice stimulates the taste buds, and the sour flavor probably masks the need for a salty taste.

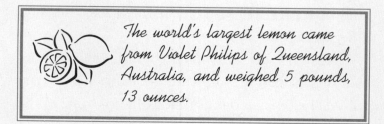

The world's largest lemon came from Violet Philips of Queensland, Australia, and weighed 5 pounds, 13 ounces.

# *Lemony Dishes*

*F*rom the soup and salad course through dessert, one can fill a multicourse meal with delicious lemony dishes. Lemon, in fact, provides the main flavoring agent in countless recipes. Of course, we all know about lemon bars and lemon meringue pie and we've been drinking lemonade since we were wee children. But many people haven't experienced the wonderful exotic flavor of a lemon-based soup, like those made by Malaysians and Greeks, to start off a meal. You'll find that lemon recipes abound for vegetable, fish, poultry, and meat dishes, in addition to a wide variety of tangy desserts that will finish off a meal like no other flavor can.

Not only do lemons taste great, but they are also one of nature's most nutritious foods. As you will see below, lemons are chock-full of some of the most important vitamins and minerals.

> *"I love lemon. It's a kick. It's an intrusion. Whenever a dish needs a little something and I'm not sure what that little something is, I start off with a squirt of lemon juice. When I need more punch, I use little chunks of seeded lemon flesh....You can be chewing away and suddenly that burst of sun in your mouth makes every other flavor shine."* —MAGGIE WALDRON

## NUTRITIONAL INFORMATION

One medium lemon or $3^{1}/_{2}$ ounces of raw lemon has 29 calories, 1 gram of protein, 9 grams of carbohydrates, and 2 grams of fiber, and contains 53 milligrams of vitamin C or 88 percent of the recommended daily allowance. Lemons, in fact, have the highest vitamin-C content of all citrus fruits. They are also rich in calcium, potassium, and magnesium as well as folic acid. Although they are acidic, it is said that their effect on the blood is alkalizing.

# Jams, Sauces, and Salad Dressings

## Lemon Marmalade

**8 lemons**
**1¹/₂ cups sugar**

1. Remove all of the lemon zest by using either a vegetable peeler, lemon zester, or a sharp paring knife, being careful not to take the pithy white part of the lemon that is immediately beneath the rind.

2. Juice the lemons and mix the juice, zest, and sugar in a large saucepan. Slowly cook over a low heat, stirring constantly for about 30 minutes, until thick and syrupy.

3. Allow the mixture to cool. It will keep for 1–2 weeks, covered, in the refrigerator.

**Makes 1 cup**

# Lemon Curd

*L*emon curd is mainly used as a spread for bread or toast, but it also makes a delicious cake or tart filling.

> *Juice of 6 lemons*
> *1 tablespoon grated lemon rind*
> *2 pounds sugar*
> *$^1/_4$ cup butter, cut into cubes*
> *6 eggs, slightly beaten*

**1.** In a large saucepan, mix lemon juice, rind, and sugar. Add butter and slightly beaten eggs and mix well. Simmer slowly over low heat, stirring steadily until the mixture thickens, for about 12 minutes.

**2.** Let stand to cool. It will be firmer when chilled. Pour the cooled mixture into sterilized pint jars with screw-top lids. Store in refrigerator.

**Makes 2 pints**

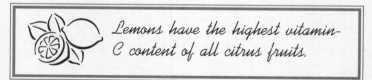 *Lemons have the highest vitamin-C content of all citrus fruits.*

# Lemon Mayonnaise

*T*his recipe works well over salads and also as a dipping sauce for fresh, whole, cooked artichokes. Try it out the next time you make a tuna or salmon salad sandwich or any other time that the recipe calls for mayonnaise.

> *2 eggs (preferably organic)*
> *5 tablespoons fresh lemon juice*
> *2 tablespoons Dijon mustard*
> *1 cup vegetable oil*
> *1 cup light olive oil*
> *Grated zest of 2 lemons*
> *Freshly ground black pepper to taste*
> *¼ cup finely chopped fresh herbs (basil,*
> *      tarragon, dill, or parsley)*

1. Blend in a mixer or food processor the eggs, lemon juice, and mustard for about 15 seconds. While the mixture is still blending, slowly add the oils and blend until the mayonnaise is thick.

2. In a bowl, lightly fold in the lemon zest and pepper and add the herbs of your choice.

**3.** Cover and refrigerate for at least 2 hours before serving.

**Makes 2¹/₂ cups**

## Gourmet Lemon Butter

*T*his recipe makes a delicious butter sauce that tops off cooked fish fillets, new potatoes, asparagus, or any other cooked vegetables.

> *1 tablespoon finely minced shallots*
> *2 tablespoons white wine vinegar*
> *1¹/₂ tablespoons dry vermouth*
> *1¹/₂ tablespoons fresh lemon juice*
> *¹/₂ cup heavy or whipping cream*
> *1 cup (2 sticks) butter, allowed to warm to*
> *    room temperature*
> *Salt and freshly ground pepper to taste*

**1.** Place the shallots, vinegar, vermouth, and lemon juice in a saucepan and cook over high heat, reducing the liquid until it has almost all evaporated.

**2.** Add the cream and lower the temperature to a medium heat and cook until the mixture has reduced and thickened slightly. Remove pan from the heat and set aside.

3. Right before you are ready to serve, place the mixture into the top of a double boiler that has warm (not hot) water inside of it. Add the butter and salt and white pepper and whisk until the butter has melted.

**Makes 1 1/2 cups**

*Oranges and lemons,*
*Say the bells of St. Clements.*
*You owe me five farthings,*
*Say the bells of St. Martins.*
*When will you pay me?*
*Say the bells of Old Bailey.*
*When I grow rich,*
*Say the bells of Shoreditch.*

—*"Oranges & Lemons"* —ANONYMOUS NURSERY RHYME

# Lemon-Mustard Salad Dressing

When you want a fresh and delicious alternative to the store-bought varieties, try this homemade dressing.

*1 egg (preferably organic)*
*1 tablespoon frozen lemonade concentrate*
*2 tablespoons fresh lemon juice*
*2 tablespoons Dijon mustard*
*2 tablespoons white wine vinegar*
*³/₄ cup extra virgin olive oil*
*Salt and freshly ground black pepper, to taste*

1. In a mixer or food processor blend the egg, lemonade concentrate, lemon juice, mustard, and vinegar for about 30 seconds.

2. Slowly add the olive oil and blend until the dressing thickens.

3. Add salt and freshly ground pepper to taste.

**Makes 1 cup**

# Soups and Salads

## Malay Lemon Rice Soup

> 1¹/₂ cups of chicken broth
> ¹/₂ cup white rice
> 1 bay leaf
> Salt (to taste, if the broth is not salted)
> ¹/₄ teaspoon summer savory
> 4 eggs, beaten
> Juice and grated peel of 2 lemons
> Fresh chopped cilantro or scallions, as garnish

**1.** Heat the chicken stock just until it boils, and add the rice, bay leaf, and salt to taste, if necessary. Simmer the mixture on low heat for approximately 30 minutes, or until the rice is thoroughly cooked. Remove the bay leaf.

**2.** Just before the rice is done, beat the eggs and mix with the summer savory. Add lemon juice and the grated lemon peel and mix again. Slowly add 1 cup of the broth to the egg mixture while continually stirring.

3. Add the egg mixture to the soup pot.

4. Before serving, add chopped cilantro or scallions as garnish for color and flavor accent.

**Serves 4**

# Greek Lemon Chicken, Orzo, and Rice Soup

*¹/₂ cup long-grained rice*
*2 quarts chicken stock*
*1 cooked, split, boneless, skinless chicken breast*
*³/₄ cup orzo*
*1 egg*
*1 egg white*
*Juice of 1¹/₂ lemons*
*Salt and freshly ground pepper to taste*
*Fresh chopped parsley, as garnish*

1. In a soup pot, bring the stock to a boil, reduce heat, and simmer with the rice for about 15 minutes.

2. While the rice and stock are simmering, rinse and pat dry the chicken breast. Salt and pepper it to

taste and sauté in a skillet in 1 tablespoon of olive oil over medium-high heat for about 4 minutes on each side, or just until done. Shred into small bite-size pieces.

3. Add the chicken pieces and orzo to the rice and simmer for another 10 minutes, until both the rice and the orzo are tender.

4. Just before serving, beat together the egg and the egg white and slowly add the lemon juice to the eggs, beating constantly. Take 1 cup of the broth from the soup pot and add to the egg mixture, beating constantly. Pour the lemon-egg broth back into the soup pot, continuing to beat the mixture.

5. Bring it all to a boil, add salt and freshly ground pepper to taste, garnish with the fresh chopped parsley, and serve immediately.

**Serves 6–8**

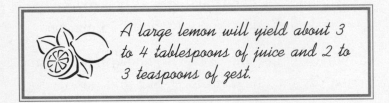

A large lemon will yield about 3 to 4 tablespoons of juice and 2 to 3 teaspoons of zest.

# Lemon-Tarragon Chicken Salad

*4 whole boneless, skinless chicken breasts*
*³/₄ cup heavy or whipping cream*
*1 head Boston lettuce*
*1 head Bibb lettuce*
*1 small head radicchio*
*1 large bunch watercress*
*1 cup walnut halves*
*2¹/₂ cups lemon mayonnaise (page 120)*
*Grated zest of 2 lemons*
*Fresh tarragon, as garnish*

1. Preheat the oven to 350 degrees Fahrenheit.

2. Wash and pat dry the chicken breasts and arrange them in a baking pan. Spread the cream evenly over the chicken. Bake for about 20 to 25 minutes until done, being careful not to over-cook.

3. While the chicken is baking, wash and dry the greens and divide into six portions arranged on individual plates.

4. After baking the chicken, remove from the oven and allow it to cool. Cut the chicken breasts into

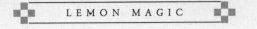

$^1/_2$- by 2-inch pieces and place on top of the greens.

5. Sprinkle the walnuts over the cut chicken. Add a spoonful of lemon mayonnaise to each serving and sprinkle a little bit of lemon zest over the servings. Finish by decorating the plates with the fresh tarragon and serve.

**Serves 6**

## *Warm Lemon Chicken Salad*

*2 whole, boneless, skinless chicken breasts*
*2 tablespoons frozen lemonade concentrate*
*2 tablespoons fresh lemon juice*
*1 cup arugula*
*1 cup romaine lettuce*
*1 cup watercress leaves*
*$^1/_2$ cup toasted almonds*
*$^1/_2$ cup toasted raisins*
*$^3/_4$ cup unbleached all-purpose flour*
*1 teaspoon paprika*
*$^1/_2$ teaspoon salt*
*$^1/_2$ teaspoon freshly ground black pepper*
*1 cup vegetable oil*
*1 cup lemon-mustard salad dressing (page 123)*

1. After thoroughly rinsing the chicken breasts and patting dry, slice them into $1/2$- by 2-inch strips and place them in a baking dish.

2. Stir the lemonade concentrate and lemon juice together and pour over the chicken. Marinate for 1 hour at room temperature, loosely covered.

3. While the chicken is marinating, prepare the salad greens. Tear the arugula and romaine into large pieces and toss together with the watercress, almonds, and raisins, and set aside.

4. Combine the flour, paprika, salt, and pepper and place in a plastic bag and shake. Then place the chicken strips in the bag and shake again, until the chicken has been thoroughly coated. Heat the oil in a skillet and fry the strips until they are crisp and golden (about 3–4 minutes on each side) and drain on paper towels.

5. Toss the greens with the lemon mustard salad dressing and divide into four portions and arrange on four plates. Place the warm chicken strips over the greens and serve immediately.

**Serves 4**

# Warm Oriental Chicken Salad in a Lemon-Sesame Sauce

*1 pound boneless, skinless chicken breast*
*4 large leaves of green or red leaf lettuce*
*1 (15 ounce) can mandarin orange segments, drained*
*¹/₄ cup soy sauce*
*1 teaspoon lemon zest*
*¹/₄ cup fresh lemon juice*
*1 tablespoon dark sesame oil*
*1 teaspoon minced garlic*
*1 teaspoon sugar*
*¹/₄ cup all-purpose unbleached flour*
*1 teaspoon sesame seeds*
*¹/₂ teaspoon freshly ground black pepper*
*1 tablespoon vegetable oil*

**1.** Combine the soy sauce, lemon zest, lemon juice, sesame oil, garlic, and sugar in a small bowl or measuring cup and stir until the sugar is dissolved. Set aside.

**2.** Place the flour, sesame seeds, and pepper in a plastic bag and shake for a moment or two. After thoroughly rinsing and patting dry the chicken breasts, cut them into $\frac{1}{2}$- by 2-inch strips and place into the bag and shake again until they are coated. Heat the vegetable oil in a skillet over medium-high heat and place the chicken strips in the pan and fry until crispy and golden, about 3 minutes on each side.

3. Place the warm chicken strips over the lettuce and ring the plate with the mandarin orange slices. Stir the lemon-sesame sauce and drizzle the dressing over the salads and serve.

**Serves 4**

*The first lemons in America were planted in St. Augustine, Florida, from a group of seeds carried to the New World by Christopher Columbus.*

# Side Dishes

## Broccoli with Lemon

*1 small- to medium-size bunch of broccoli*
*2 tablespoons of butter*
*Juice of half a lemon*
*Salt and freshly ground pepper to taste*

**1.** After cleaning the broccoli, cut and trim the vegetable into flowerettes, discarding the thickest portion of the stem. Steam or boil the broccoli for 3–4 minutes until the vegetable is tender.

**2.** While the broccoli is cooking, heat the butter in a saucepan over low heat and add the lemon juice. Remove the broccoli from the steamer (or drain the water from the broccoli if it has been boiled) and drizzle the lemon butter over the broccoli.

**3.** Sprinkle with salt and freshly ground pepper and serve.

**Serves 4**

# String Beans with Lemon & Parsley

*1 pound green beans, ends trimmed and cut into*
*    2-inch pieces*
*2 tablespoons of butter at room temperature*
*Juice of ¹/₂ lemon*
*2 tablespoons finely chopped parsley*
*Salt and freshly ground pepper to taste*

1. After chopping the beans, rinse and drain. Either place the beans in a steamer or in a pan with water to cover and steam or simmer for about 10 minutes, or until tender.

2. Drain beans and return to saucepan. Add the room temperature butter and drizzle the lemon juice over the beans and add the chopped parsley, salt, and pepper. Toss mixture together and serve while still hot.

**Serves 4**

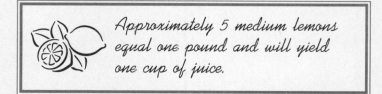 *Approximately 5 medium lemons equal one pound and will yield one cup of juice.*

# Zucchini with Olive Oil, Oregano, and Lemon

*2 or 3 zucchini (about 1³/₄ pounds)*
*3 tablespoons extra virgin olive oil*
*Juice of ¹/₂ lemon*
*Salt and freshly ground pepper to taste*

**1.** Clean and trim the ends of the zucchini. Cut the vegetables into pieces that are about 1 inch wide and 2 inches in length.

**2.** Heat the olive oil in a skillet and add the zucchini, salt, and freshly ground pepper. Cook over medium heat, shaking and stirring the zucchini around in the pan until its color starts to intensify.

**3.** Add the lemon juice and cover, cooking for about 3 minutes or just until crisp. Serve immediately.

**Serves 4**

# Main Courses: Pasta, Fish, and Meat

## Penne and Spring Vegetables in Lemon-Thyme Sauce

2 tablespoons virgin olive oil

1 medium onion, chopped

1–2 cloves of garlic, minced

³/₄ cup broccoli flowerettes

³/₄ cup freshly shelled peas

³/₄ cup asparagus pieces

³/₄ cup thinly sliced carrots

³/₄ cup of chicken or vegetable stock

Juice of ¹/₂ lemon

1 teaspoon grated lemon rind

1¹/₂ teaspoons of dried thyme or a few sprigs of
    fresh thyme with woody parts removed

4 ounces penne pasta, cooked

Freshly ground parmesan cheese

Salt and freshly ground pepper to taste

Flat-leafed Italian parsley, optional garnish

1. Heat the olive oil in a large saucepan over medium heat and sauté the onions and garlic until the onions are transparent. If using dried thyme, add while onions and garlic are cooking; if using fresh thyme, add later.

2. Add the chicken or vegetable stock, lemon rind, and lemon juice and simmer uncovered until the sauce is somewhat reduced, about 5 minutes.

3. Add the chopped vegetables and cook over medium heat for about 5 minutes or until tender. Add the fresh thyme once the vegetables have been cooked.

4. Add the penne, cooked al dente, to the saucepan and toss together, adding salt, pepper, and parmesan cheese to taste before serving. Add parsley to the plates as garnish if desired.

**Serves 4**

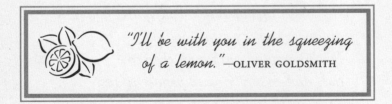

*"I'll be with you in the squeezing of a lemon."* —OLIVER GOLDSMITH

# Lemon Chive Pasta

*T*his simple pasta recipe makes for a delicious accompaniment to grilled fish, chicken, or meat dishes.

> *4 ounces dry pasta (farfalle, spinach or tomato*
>     *fettuccine, or orzo)*
> *2 tablespoons butter or virgin olive oil*
> *¹/₄ cup finely chopped chives*
> *1 teaspoon finely shredded lemon peel*
> *Salt and freshly ground pepper to taste*

1. Cook the pasta until it is al dente and drain well.

2. Melt the butter or heat the olive oil in a large saucepan and add the lemon rind and the chives.

3. Add the cooked pasta to the lemon butter (or oil) and toss. Add salt to taste, freshly ground pepper, and serve.

**Serves 4**

# Lemon Grouper in Tomato-Rosemary Sauce

*1¹/₄ pound grouper fillet*
*³/₄ cup diced plum tomatoes*
*1 teaspoon minced garlic*
*1¹/₂ teaspoons fresh lemon juice*
*¹/₂ teaspoon Worcestershire sauce*
*2 dashes hot sauce (Tabasco, habanero or your*
    *favorite hot sauce)*
*2 teaspoons chopped fresh rosemary or*
    *³/₄ teaspoon dried rosemary*
*1 large lemon, thinly sliced crosswise*
*Salt and freshly ground pepper to taste*

**1.** Preheat oven to 450 degrees Fahrenheit.

**2.** Combine the tomatoes, garlic, lemon juice, Worcestershire sauce, hot sauce, and salt and pepper in a blender or food processor. Once the mixture is blended, add the rosemary and mix well.

**3.** Line a lightly greased baking dish with the lemon slices arranged in the shape of the grouper fillet, and after rinsing and drying the fish, place it on top of the lemon slices. Bake, covered, for 15–20 minutes.

**Serves 4**

## Sautéed Flounder in Lemon Sauce

*1¼ pound of flounder, filleted in 4 pieces*
*¼ cup dried bread crumbs*
*2 tablespoons olive oil*
*½ cup dry white wine*
*1 teaspoon minced garlic*
*2 tablespoons fresh lemon juice*
*1 tablespoon orange juice*
*1 teaspoon butter*
*2 tablespoons chopped fresh chives*
*Salt and freshly ground pepper to taste*

1. Add salt and pepper to taste to the bread crumbs and place the bread crumbs in a shallow bowl that is big enough to hold one of the fillets at a time. Coat each fillet and set aside for a moment.

2. Heat the olive oil in a large skillet and sauté the fillets for 2 minutes on each side or until

browned on medium-high heat. Remove the fish and place on a platter and cover.

3. Add the wine, garlic, lemon juice, and orange juice to the pan and cook on high heat for about a minute until the mixture becomes slightly thickened. Add the scallions and remove the pan from the heat and stir in the butter.

4. Pour the sauce over the fish and then sprinkle each portion with a small amount of chives and serve.

**Serves 4**

## *Seviche*

> *2 pounds raw bay scallops*
> *1 fresh hot red pepper, julienned*
> *1 small sweet red pepper, julienned*
> *¹/₂ small purple onion, julienned*
> *2 ripe tomatoes, seeded, chopped, cut into*
>  *¹/₄-inch cubes*
> *1 garlic clove, finely minced*
> *2 teaspoons brown sugar*
> *2 tablespoons chopped fresh parsley*

*2 cups fresh lime juice*
*¹/₂ cup fresh lemon juice*
*2 avocados, peeled and cut into 16 slices,*
*    brushed with lemon juice*
*Freshly chopped parsley*
*Salt and freshly ground pepper to taste*

**1.** Combine all the ingredients in a large bowl except for the avocados and the parsley, which will be used for a garnish. Gently but thoroughly toss, making certain that the lemon and lime juice coats the raw scallops.

**2.** Cover the bowl with plastic wrap and refrigerate for at least 5 hours, or until the scallops lose their translucent appearance and appear to be "cooked."

**3.** Serve in individual bowls, garnished with the avocado slices and chopped parsley. Be sure to coat the avocado slices with fresh lemon juice beforehand so they will retain their bright green color.

**Serves 8 appetizer portions**

# Baked Lemon Salmon Fillet

*1³/4 pounds salmon fillet*
*Vegetable oil spray*
*1 lemon, very thinly sliced crosswise, seeds*
 *removed*
*1 large white onion or yellow onion, very thinly*
 *sliced crosswise*
*Salt and freshly ground pepper to taste*

**1.** Heat the oven to 450 degrees Fahrenheit.

**2.** Place the salmon fillet in a baking pan that has been lightly coated with vegetable oil. Spray the fillet with the vegetable oil and sprinkle it with salt and freshly ground pepper.

**3.** Place the thin lemon slices on the fillet and the thin onion slices on top and place the baking dish in the oven and bake for about 20 minutes, or until the fish is cooked throughout.

**Serves 2**

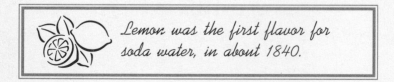

*Lemon was the first flavor for soda water, in about 1840.*

# Broiled Sea Bass with Lemon-Dill Marinade

*6 6-ounce, $^1/_2$-inch fillets of sea bass*
*$^1/_3$ cup virgin olive oil*
*2 tablespoons dry vermouth*
*1 tablespoon minced garlic*
*2 tablespoons lemon pulp, membranes and skin discarded*
*2 tablespoons fresh chives*
*2 tablespoons fresh Italian parsley*
*2 tablespoons minced fresh dill*
*1 tablespoon kosher salt*
*$^1/_2$ teaspoon freshly ground pepper*

1. Place all the ingredients in a blender or food processor and blend for about a minute.

2. Place the fish fillets in a shallow dish and spoon the marinade completely over both sides of the fish. Cover and allow to marinate for about a half hour.

3. Broil the fish fillets 4-5 inches from the broiler flame for 5–8 minutes, or until they are lightly browned and cooked throughout.

**Serves 6**

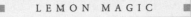

# Broiled Chicken in a Lemon-Herb Sauce

*2 pounds whole chicken pieces (dark or white meat)*
*2 tablespoons vegetable oil*
*1 tablespoon Dijon mustard*
*1 tablespoon lemon juice*
*1¹/₂ teaspoons lemon-pepper seasoning*
*1 teaspoon dried oregano or basil (crushed)*
*¹/₄ teaspoon onion salt*
*¹/₈ teaspoon red pepper*
*Fresh basil or oregano as a garnish*

1. Rinse the chicken pieces and pat dry and place them skin-side down in a broiler pan. Broil the chicken for about 20 minutes at a distance of 4–5 inches from the broiler flame.

2. While the chicken is cooking, combine the vegetable oil, Dijon mustard, lemon juice, lemon-pepper seasoning, oregano or basil, salt and red pepper in a small bowl and mix thoroughly.

3. After the chicken has cooked, brush the pieces with the lemon-mustard glaze and turn, brush once more, and broil skin-side up for another

10–15 minutes (or until it is no longer pink). Brush often with the glaze during the last 5 minutes of cooking.

4. Garnish with fresh basil or oregano leaves and serve

**Serves 4–6**

## Lemon-Marinated Steak

> 1 1½ pound beef chuck steak, cut about 1 inch thick
> 1 teaspoon finely shredded lemon peel
> ⅓ cup lemon juice
> ¼ cup vegetable oil
> ¼ cup chopped onion
> 1 tablespoon sugar
> 1 tablespoon Worcestershire sauce
> 1 teaspoon Dijon mustard
> Salt and pepper

1. After trimming the fat from the meat, place in a plastic bag set in a shallow dish. Combine the lemon peel, lemon juice, vegetable oil, onion, sugar, Worcestershire sauce, mustard, ¼ teaspoon salt, and ¼ teaspoon pepper in a small

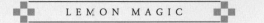

bowl and stir until it is mixed. Pour this marinade sauce into the bag with the chuck steak and marinate in the refrigerator for 6–24 hours, turning occasionally.

2. After the beef has marinated, remove it from the bag, reserving the marinade juices, and place in a broiling pan. Broil the meat 3 inches from the broiling flame for about 6 minutes on each side (or until desired doneness), turning once and rebrushing with the reserved marinade sauce. If you want to barbecue, grill the steak for about 9 minutes on each side for medium-cooked meat.

**Serves 4–6**

# Desserts

## Lemon Sorbet

*4 large thick-skinned lemons*
*2 cups sugar*
*2 cups water*
*4 fresh mint leaves*

1. Cut a cap off the stem end of each lemon and set them aside.

2. Using a grapefruit spoon, scoop out the flesh, taking care not to pierce the peel. Place the lemon shells and the caps in the freezer.

3. In a blender, puree the lemon pulp.

4. In a saucepan, dissolve the sugar in the water over low heat. Remove the syrup from the heat and set it aside to cool.

5. Mix the pureed pulp with the syrup, and freeze the mixture for about 3 hours, or until it forms a sorbet.

6. Fill the frozen, hollowed-out lemon shells with the sorbet and cover with the caps. Garnish with

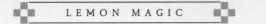
a leaf of fresh mint and keep in the freezer until serving time.

**Serves 4**

## *Lemon Bars*

*¹/₃ cup margarine or butter*
*1 cup sugar*
*1 cup plus 2 tablespoons all-purpose flour*
*2 eggs*
*2 teaspoons finely shredded lemon peel*
*3 tablespoons lemon juice*
*¹/₄ teaspoon baking powder*
*Powdered sugar*

1. Preheat oven to 350 degrees Fahrenheit.

2. In an electric mixer, beat the margarine or butter at medium-high speed for about 30 seconds and add ¹/₄ cup sugar until the mixture is combined. With the mixer still running, add 1 cup of the flour until the mixture has a crumbly texture.

3. Press the blended mixture into the bottom of an ungreased 8 x 8 x 2–inch baking pan and bake in the oven until golden (about 15–18 minutes).

**4.** While the bottom crust is baking, mix the eggs, remaining sugar, 2 tablespoons flour, lemon peel, juice, and baking powder and beat for 2 minutes until thoroughly combined.

**5.** Remove the pan from the oven and pour the blended egg mixture over the hot, baked layer. Keep the oven set at 350 degrees and replace the pan in the oven and bake for about 20 minutes until it has set and the edges are slightly golden brown.

**6.** Cool on a rack and cut into bars. Lightly dust a little powdered sugar over bars and serve.

**Makes 20 portions**

*When lemons are picked ripe, they are sweet and only slightly acidic. For this reason, commercially sold lemons are usually harvested when green and left to ripen artificially in warehouses for 1 to 4 months.*

# Lemon Pudding Cake

*$^1/_2$ cup sugar*
*3 tablespoons all-purpose flour*
*1 teaspoon finely shredded lemon peel*
*3 tablespoons lemon juice*
*2 tablespoons margarine, melted*
*2 slightly beaten egg yolks*
*1 cup milk*
*2 egg whites*

1. Preheat the oven to 350 degrees Fahrenheit.

2. Mix together the sugar and flour and then stir in the lemon peel, lemon juice, and melted margarine. In a separate bowl, combine the egg yolks and the milk and add to the flour mixture and stir until combined.

3. Beat the egg whites until stiff and gently fold into the lemon batter.

4. Transfer the mixture to a 1-quart casserole dish and place in a larger pan on an oven rack. Add hot water to the larger pan to a depth of 1 inch and bake for about 40 minutes or till golden and the top of the cake gently springs back when touched.

**Serves 4**

# Lemon Poppyseed Cake

$^1/_2$ cup butter

1 cup sugar

1 teaspoon vanilla

3 eggs

$^1/_2$ cup lemon yogurt

$1^1/_2$ cups all-purpose flour

$^1/_4$ teaspoon baking powder

$^1/_8$ teaspoon baking soda

1 teaspoons finely shredded lemon peel

2 tablespoons lemon juice

2 tablespoons poppy seeds

1. Preheat oven to 325 degrees Fahrenheit.

2. Leave out $^1/_3$ cup butter, 3 eggs, and $^1/_2$ cup yogurt until they are at room temperature.

3. Beat the butter in an electric mixer on medium-high speed for about 30 seconds and gradually add 1 cup sugar, beating about 10 minutes or until very light and fluffy. Add 1 teaspoon vanilla and the eggs, one at a time, beating 1 minute after each addition and scraping the bowl often.

4. In a separate bowl, combine $1^1/_2$ cups all-

151

purpose flour, $1/4$ teaspoon baking powder, and $1/8$ teaspoon baking soda together.

5. Add the flour mixture and the lemon yogurt alternately to the butter and egg mixture, blending it on a low to medium speed after each addition.

6. Add 1 teaspoon finely shredded lemon peel, 2 tablespoons lemon juice, and 2 tablespoons poppy seeds to the batter, mix well and pour into a greased and floured 8 x 4 x 2– or 9 x 5 x 3–inch loaf pan.

7. Bake for 60 to 75 minutes or till a toothpick comes out clean. Cool on rack, remove from pan.

**Serves 10**

There is a belief among musicians that if you suck a lemon within sight of a trumpeter, his lips will pucker up to such an extent that he will be unable to play.

# Lemon Meringue Pie

*Filling:*
 *1¹/₂ cups sugar*
 *3 tablespoons all-purpose flour*
 *3 tablespoons cornstarch*
 *3 eggs*
 *2 tablespoons margarine or butter*
 *1–2 teaspoons finely shredded lemon peel*
 *¹/₃ cup lemon juice*
 *Baked pie pastry shell*
*Meringue:*
 *3 egg whites*
 *¹/₂ teaspoon vanilla*
 *¹/₄ teaspoon cream of tartar*
 *6 tablespoons sugar*

1. Preheat oven to 350 degrees Fahrenheit.

2. **For the pie filling:** In a medium saucepan, combine sugar, flour, cornstarch, and a dash of salt. Gradually stir in 1¹/₂ cups water and cook and stir over a medium-high heat until the mixture is thick and bubbly. Reduce the heat and stir for another 2 minutes on the lowered heat and remove the pan from the stove.

3. Separate the egg whites from the egg yolks, sav-

ing the whites for the meringue portion of the recipe. Slightly beat the yolks and slowly stir in 1 cup of the hot filling and return the mixture to the saucepan and bring to a gentle boil, stirring for 2 minutes more before removing from heat.

4. Stir in the margarine and the lemon peel. Stir in the lemon juice slowly, mixing thoroughly, and pour into a baked pie or pastry shell.

5. Have the ingredients all together for the meringue portion of the recipe so you can quickly spread the meringue over the hot pie filling before baking.

1. **For the meringue:** Allow the egg whites to come to room temperature and in a mixing bowl combine the egg whites, vanilla, and cream of tartar.

2. Beat with an electric mixer on a medium speed about 1 minute or till soft peaks form. Gradually add sugar, 1 tablespoon at a time, beating on high speed about 4 minutes more or until the mixture forms stiff, glossy peaks and the sugar dissolves.

3. Quickly spread the meringue over the pie and bake for 15 minutes. Cool on a rack, cover, and chill to store.

**Serves 8**

# Honey-Baked Pears in Lemon Sauce

*Lemon Sauce:*
>    1 tablespoon arrowroot powder
>    1$^1$/$_2$ cups milk
>    1 stick cinnamon
>    Grated rind of 2 lemons
>    $^1$/$_4$ cup fresh lemon juice
>    $^1$/$_4$ cup honey

*Pears:*
>    6 ripe but firm pears
>    $^1$/$_4$ cup honey
>    $^1$/$_2$ cup water
>    4 or 5 whole cloves

1. Preheat oven to 350 degrees Fahrenheit.

2. To make the lemon sauce, start by dissolving the arrowroot powder in $^1$/$_4$ cup of the milk and lace it into a saucepan with the remaining milk and cinnamon. Stir and cook over low heat until slightly thickened.

3. Add lemon rind, lemon juice, and honey. Remove from heat, cover, and chill in the refrig-

erator. Just before serving time, remove the cinnamon and pour the sauce over the pears.

4. Wash and cut the pears in half lengthwise, remove the core and seeds, and place pears in a glass baking dish.

5. Bring the honey, water, and cloves in a small saucepan to the point of boiling. Remove from heat and pour the mixture over the pears. Bake for 10 to 15 minutes or just until the pears are tender, being careful not to overcook them. Serve warm with chilled lemon sauce.

**Makes 6 portions**

# Bibliography

## BOOKS

*Baking Soda: Over 500 Fabulous, Fun, and Frugal Uses You've Probably Never Thought Of,* Vicky Lansky. Deephaven, Minnesota: The Book Peddlers, 1995.

*Better Homes and Gardens New Cook Book,* eds. Jennifer Darling, Linda Henry, Rosemary C. Hutchinson, and Mary Major. Des Moines, Iowa: Meredith Corporation, 1989.

*Bug Busters: Getting Rid of Household Pests Without Dangerous Chemicals,* Bernice Lifton. New York: McGraw Hill, 1985.

*Can You Trust a Tomato in January?,* Vince Staten. New York: Simon & Schuster, 1993.

*Chicken Soup and Other Folk Remedies,* Joan Wilen and Lydia Wilen. New York: Fawcett Columbine, 1984.

*The Citrus Cookbook,* Josephine Bacon. Boston: Harvard Common Press, 1983.

*Clean and Green: The Complete Guide to Nontoxic and Environmentally Safe Housekeeping,* Annie Berthold-Bond. Woodstock, NY: Ceres Press, 1990.

*The Complete Home Health Advisor,* Rita Elkins. Pleasant Grove, Utah: Woodland Health Books, 1994.

*The Deaf Smith Country Cookbook,* Marjorie Winn Ford, Susan Hillyard, and Mary Faulk Koock. New York: Collier Books, 1973.

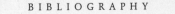
*The Doctor's Book of Home Remedies II,* Sid Kirchheimer. Emmaus, Pennsylvania: Rodale Press, 1993.

*Don Aslett's Stainbuster's Bible: The Complete Guide to Spot Removal,* Don Aslett. New York: Plume, 1990.

*Eater's Choice: A Food Lover's Guide to Lower Cholesterol,* Ron Goor and Nancy Goor. Boston: Houghton Mifflin Company, 1992.

*Fashionable Food: Seven Decades of Food Fads,* Sylvia Lovegren. New York: Macmillan, 1995.

*The Fastest, Cheapest, Best Way to Clean Everything,* Editors of Consumer Guide®. New York: Simon & Schuster, 1980.

*Food,* Waverly Root. New York: Simon & Schuster, 1980.

*Food in History,* Reay Tannahill. New York: Crown Publishers, 1989.

*Home Remedies: What Works,* Gale Maleskey and Brian Kaufman. Emmaus, Pennsylvania: Rodale Press, 1995.

*Home Safe Home,* Debra Lynn Dadd. New York: Jeremy Tarcher, 1997.

*Household Hints and Handy Tips,* Reader's Digest. Pleasantville, New York: Reader's Digest Association, 1988.

*If I'd Only Listened to My Mom, I'd Know How to Do This: Hundreds of Household Remedies,* Jean B. MacLeod. New York: St. Martin's Griffin, 1997.

*The Illustrated Book of Signs and Symbols,* Miranda Bruce-Mitford. New York: Dorling Kindersley, 1996.

*Jane Brody's Good Seafood Book,* Jane Brody. New York: Fawcett Columbine, 1994.

*Mary Ellen's Complete Home Reference Book,* Mary Ellen Pinkham. New York: Crown Trade Paperbacks, 1993.

*Mythology,* Edith Hamilton. Boston: Little Brown, 1942.

*Never Eat More Than You Can Lift and Other Food Quotes and Quips,* Sharon Tyler Herbst. New York: Broadway Books, 1997.

*The New Basics Cookbook,* Julee Rosso and Sheila Lukins. New York: Workman Publishing, 1989.

*The Pantropheon or A History of Food and Its Preparation in Ancient Times,* Alexis Soyer. New York: Paddington Press, 1977.

*Polly's Pointers: 1081 Helpful Hints for Making Everything Last Longer,* Polly Fisher. New York: Rawson Wade Publishers, 1981.

*Savannah Seasons: Food and Stories from Elizabeth on 37th,* Elizabeth Terry. New York: Doubleday, 1996.

*The Scented House,* Penny Black. New York: Simon and Schuster, 1990.

*The Silver Palate Cookbook,* Julee Rosso and Sheila Lukins. New York: Workman Publishing, 1982.

*60-Minute Gourmet,* Pierre Franey. New York: Fawcett Columbine, 1979.

*6001 Food Facts and Chef's Secrets,* Myles H. Bader. Las Vegas: Northstar Publishing Company, 1995.

## WEBSITES

www.mamagaia.com/mgocleaning.htm

www.healthcaresources.com/helpfulhints.htm

www.laughingbird.com/mega_tips/cookingtips.html

# *Index*